THE FIRST BATTLE OF
NEWBURY

THE FIRST BATTLE OF
NEWBURY

JOHN BARRATT

TEMPUS

This edition first published 2005

Tempus Publishing Limited
The Mill, Brimscombe Port,
Stroud, Gloucestershire, GL5 2QG
www.tempus-publishing.com

© John Barratt, 2005

The right of John Barratt to be identified as the Author
of this work has been asserted in accordance with the
Copyrights, Designs and Patents Act 1988.

All rights reserved. No part of this book may be reprinted
or reproduced or utilised in any form or by any electronic,
mechanical or other means, now known or hereafter invented,
including photocopying and recording, or in any information
storage or retrieval system, without the permission in writing
from the Publishers.

British Library Cataloguing in Publication Data.
A catalogue record for this book is available from the British Library.

ISBN 0 7524 2569 2

Typesetting and origination by Tempus Publishing Limited.
Printed in Great Britain.

Contents

About the Author		6
Preface		7
Chronology		9
1	The Strategic Situation: Summer 1643	11
2	The Siege of Gloucester: August–September 1643	21
3	The Race for Newbury: 7–19 September 1643	39
4	The Armies	71
5	Newbury: Approach to Battle	83
6	Newbury: The Battle	95
7	Aftermath	111
Notes		139
Appendix: Order of Battle		143
Bibliography		147
List of Illustrations		149
Index		153

About the Author

John Barratt has written and lectured extensively on the English Civil War. His other books include *The Battle for York: Marston Moor 1644*, *The Great Siege of Chester* (both published by Tempus), *Cavaliers: The Royalist Army at War 1642–46* and *Cavalier Generals: King Charles I & His Commanders*. He also writes regularly for *Military Illustrated* and *The English Civil War Times*. He lectures at the National Army Museum and the Royal Armories. He lives on Merseyside.

Preface

By the summer of 1643 the Royalist tide of success in the English Civil War was approaching its peak. The capture of Bristol, England's second largest port, on 26 July climaxed a string of successes which had seen most of the west and north of England pass into the King's control. The Royalists appeared to be on the verge of complete victory, with one more major reverse likely to bring the tottering Parliamentarian cause crashing down.

The Royalist Council of War hoped to make the capture of the town of Gloucester that catalyst. But the siege which followed, together with its succeeding campaign climaxing in the First Battle of Newbury (20 September), proved instead to be decisive in thwarting the hopes of the Cavaliers. Though the King's supporters would enjoy other successes in the following weeks, their hopes of decisive victory faded into a military stalemate in which the growing power of the Parliamentarian-Scots alliance would eventually tip the scales inexorably in favour of the King's opponents.

Though its significance was not fully grasped at the time, the First Battle of Newbury, variously regarded as indecisive, a Royalist failure or a narrow victory for the Parliamentarians under the Earl of Essex, was far-reaching in its effects. By avoiding a defeat which would have almost certainly have been fatal for his cause, 'Old Robin' as Essex was known to his troops, not only saved his army but breathed decisive new life into the Parliamentarians.

Despite its importance and its ranking, in terms of numbers involved, as probably the third largest battle of the First Civil War, Newbury is one of the more neglected actions of the conflict. Indeed the battlefield itself lacks much of the visual interest of, for example, the other great engagements at Edgehill and Marston Moor. A large part of it is now covered by the spreading suburban housing of the modern town of Newbury, whose roads, named after such luminaries of the action as Cary, Villiers and Essex, represent the only visible reminders on much of the battlefield. Further dislocation has resulted in recent years from the development of the controversial Newbury bypass, while the only monument, a nineteenth-century memorial to the Earl of Falkland, stands marooned on a small grassy island amidst a busy road intersection some distance from the probable site of his death.

Only on the northern part of the battlefield, around the key high ground now known as Round Hill, and in some of its adjacent high-banked lanes, does the modern terrain still give an idea of its significance and appearance in 1643.

To add to the difficulties encountered by anyone attempting to reconstruct the course of what has been described as 'a monumentally confusing' battle, extant contemporary accounts give little information regarding many of its details. Yet Newbury's significance is such that it deserves much fuller treatment than is usually afforded to it.

As in previous books, I owe a great debt of gratitude to the painstaking researches of many others in the field of the English Civil War and of seventeenth-century military theory and practice. Among them are David Blackmore, David Evans, John Lewis, Les Prince, Stuart Reid, Keith Roberts, David Ryan, John Tincey and the late Brigadier Peter Young, whose enthusiasm and pioneering research did so much to spark the modern interest in the Civil Wars.

As usual, I owe a great deal to the long-suffering and invariably helpful staff of a number of libraries, including the Sydney Jones Library, University of Liverpool; Berkshire County Libraries and Record Office; the British Library, London, and the Bodleian Library, Oxford. At Tempus Publishing, Jonathan Reeve and Joanna Lincoln and their team have provided their customary outstanding support.

John Barratt, April 2003

Chronology

1642

22 August — King Charles I raises Royal Standard at Nottingham, signalling formal outbreak of Civil War.

23 October — Battle of Edgehill. Marginal victory for Royalists over Earl of Essex.

12 November — Royalist advance on London checked at Turnham Green.

9 December — Royalists go into winter quarters around temporary capital of Oxford.

1643

19 January — Battle of Braddock Down. Cornish Royalists under Sir Ralph Hopton defeat Parliamentarian invasion of Cornwall.

15–27 April — Essex takes Reading.

16 May — Hopton defeats Parliamentarian army under Earl of Stamford at Stratton, decisively winning battle for Cornwall.

18 June — Prince Rupert defeats Parliamentarian cavalry at Chalgrove. John Hampden mortally wounded. Essex's campaign in Thames Valley stalled by sickness among troops.

30 June — Northern Royalists under Earl of Newcastle win major victory over Parliamentarian army of Lord Fairfax at Adwalton Moor.

5 July — Battle of Lansdown. Parliamentarian army under Sir William Waller narrowly defeats Western Royalists under Marquis of Hertford and Hopton.

13 July — Battle of Roundway Down. Cavalry force under Lord Wilmot and Sir John Byron defeat Waller and relieve Hopton, besieged in Devizes. Queen's munitions convoy reaches Oxford, enabling Oxford Army to begin active operations.

26 July — Prince Rupert storms Bristol.

4 August — Royalist Council of War decides to besiege Gloucester.

10 August — Siege of Gloucester begins.

19 August	Parliament requests City of London to provide troops from London Trained Bands to reinforce Essex in relief march.
23 August	Trained Bands set out from London.
24 August	Essex begins relief march.
31 August	Skirmish between Sir Philip Stapleton and Royalist horse from Banbury.
1 September	General rendezvous of Essex's army and London Brigade on Brackley Heath. Action between John Middleton and Royalist horse under Lord Wilmot at Deddington.
3 September	Parliamentarians reach Stow-on-the-Wold.
4 September	Rupert fails to check Essex at Stow-on-the-Wold.
5 September	Royalists raise siege at Gloucester.
8 September	Essex enters Gloucester; Royalists move to Evesham, blocking road to London.
10 September	Essex marches to Tewkesbury.
15 September	Essex begins return march to London.
16 September	Essex surprises Royalist convoy at Cirencester; Rupert and King begin pursuit of Essex.
17 September	Essex at Swindon; Rupert at Faringdon; King at Northleach.
18 September	Action at Aldbourne Chase; Rupert slows Essex's march.
19 September	Royalists reach Newbury ahead of Essex, blocking road to London.
20 September	Battle of Newbury.
21 September	Essex resumes march and beats off attack on rearguard by Rupert at Aldermaston.
22 September	King returns to Oxford; Essex reaches Reading.
25 September	Essex reaches London; army quarters at Windsor.
28 September	Essex's triumphal entry into London.

I

The Strategic Situation Summer 1643

By the early summer of 1643 the tide of military success in the English Civil War seemed to be flowing increasingly in favour of the Royalists. Nearly a year of conflict had brought varying fortunes for both sides. The autumn campaign of 1642, which many had expected to bring a quick decision to the war, had given King Charles I a narrow victory at Edgehill (23 October) in the first major engagement of the war. But, probably correctly, the King and his Council of War had vetoed a plan by Charles' nephew and General of Horse, the twenty-three-year-old Prince Rupert, to make a dash for London with a flying column of cavalry and mounted musketeers. Instead the Royalists had opted for the safer course of a more methodical advance on the capital.

The outcome in early November was a stand-off between the opposing armies of King Charles and the Parliamentarian Captain-General, Robert Devereux, 2nd Earl of Essex, at Turnham Green on the approaches to London. Unwilling to risk an engagement with the strongly positioned Parliamentarians, the Royalists had fallen back, establishing their headquarters and temporary capital at Oxford, while both sides prepared for a prolonged war.

During the winter, most parts of England and Wales were caught up, to a greater or lesser extent, in the spreading conflict. The opening months of 1643 saw the honours of war distributed fairly evenly. The Parliamentarians held their own in the vital Thames Valley area, and gained ground in north-west England and the West Midlands. For their part the Cavaliers could gain satisfaction from holding their own in Cornwall and the north-east, and the King's forces had expanded the area under their control around Oxford, where Rupert and his cavalry were burnishing their reputation with a number of minor successes.

The arrival of spring saw a stepping-up in the pace of operations. Although in the long term the Parliamentarians' greater resources of men, money and materials would increasingly make themselves felt, in the spring and early summer of 1643, the Royalist armies, invigorated by new recruits and supplies of munitions imported from the Continent, enjoyed a steady stream of successes.

Prince Rupert, in a lightning operation in the West Midlands, sacked Birmingham and captured Lichfield, improving Royalist communications with the north. However in the Thames Valley, following an initial success in taking Reading, the Earl of Essex made slow progress. Intended operations against Oxford were crippled by Essex's caution, the ravages of disease and desertion among his troops and the effective counter-strikes by the Royalist cavalry, climaxing in Rupert's victory at Chalgrove (18 June).

Although the King's opponents continued to gain ground in Lancashire and Cheshire, elsewhere in the north Royalist forces under the Earl of Newcastle, supplied with arms and ammunition from the Low Countries, increasingly gained the upper hand over the smaller northern Parliamentarian army led by Lord Fairfax and his son, Sir Thomas. On 30 June, Newcastle gained a crushing victory over the Fairfaxes at Adwalton Moor near Bradford. The remnants of the northern Parliamentarian forces were forced to seek refuge behind the strong defences of the port of Hull, apparently leaving the way open for Newcastle and his 'Popish Army' to drive on into the heartlands of the Parliamentarian Eastern Association.

In the south-west also, after initially fluctuating fortunes, the Cavaliers were meeting with increasing success. The largely Cornish Royalist army led by Sir Ralph Hopton advanced eastwards through Devon, and in June linked up in Somerset with troops from Oxford under the King's Lieutenant-General in the west, the Marquis of Hertford, and Rupert's younger brother, Prince Maurice. A closely contested duel with the Parliamentarian army of Sir William Waller followed. The opponents were well matched in skill and strength, and for some time the issue remained in doubt. Following cavalry skirmishes in the Mendip hills, the main armies clashed on 5 July on Lansdown Hill, outside Bath. In assaulting Waller's strong defensive position the Cavaliers suffered heavy casualties, especially among their Cornish infantry. The contest ended at nightfall with no clear victor, but with the battered Royalists pulling back and heading eastwards towards the town of Devizes, hoping to gain assistance from Oxford.

Waller, dogging their footsteps, besieged the Royalist foot in Devizes, but their horse broke out and, linking up with reinforcements from Oxford under the King's Lieutenant-General of Horse, Lord Wilmot, and Sir John Byron, returned to inflict a crushing defeat on Waller outside Devizes on Roundway Down (12 July).

The battle left the Parliamentarians without any effective field army in the west of England, and the Royalists were free to turn their attention to the great prize of the city of Bristol, England's second port and an important trading and manufacturing centre. Rupert had been frustrated in an attempt to take control of Bristol by means of treachery earlier in the year, and this time was determined to make sure of success. He reinforced the Western Royalist forces with a major part of the Oxford Army and on 26 July, in a fiercely contested action, stormed Bristol.

England's second city was now in the King's hands, though Royalist casualties had been heavy, especially among the Cornish infantry, whose losses of 500 rank and file and many officers greatly reduced their effectiveness for a considerable time to come. Nonetheless, few doubted that the price had been worth paying. By the beginning of August 1643 the Royalists appeared clearly dominant in every strategically important theatre of the war, and, with the only remaining major opposing army, that of the Earl of Essex, still seriously under-strength and with sagging morale, it seemed that one more major defeat might be sufficient to bring down the Parliamentarian cause.

For the Royalists the overriding question was how to strike such a decisive blow. The Cavaliers were far from certain as to their best next course of action. It was clear that the war had entered a critical phase, and the resolutions which the King and his advisers now reached might well settle its outcome. Unfortunately, a number of weaknesses in the Royalist position presented problems at a time when speed and decisiveness were vital.

There were divisions and rivalry among the leadership on both sides and, unfortunately for the Royalists, the period immediately following the capture of Bristol was one of the occasions on which they made themselves apparent among the Royalist commanders. Losses at Bristol, totalling perhaps 1,000 men, as well as the large expenditure of powder and ammunition incurred in the storming, were themselves enough to cause a delay in operations, but the situation was exacerbated by disagreements in the Royalist high command. As was not unusual, much of the fault seems to lie with the tactless and high-handed behaviour of Prince Rupert, who without reference to the Marquis of Hertford, nominally the senior commander in the west, had written to the King asking to be appointed as Governor of Bristol. Hertford had already given the job to Hopton, and only after some haggling was the situation resolved when Hopton was made Lieutenant-Governor under Rupert, and in practice placed in day-to-day command at Bristol, with Hertford 'honourably retired' to the court at Oxford. The dispute apparently required the King's personal presence in order to be resolved. However, other than demonstrating the divisions which dogged the Royalist leadership, it is unlikely that it actually did much to delay operations, as the Royalist army was in any case barely fit for immediate action because of the casualties it had incurred in storming Bristol and the large numbers of troops who had deserted with their booty.

On 1 August Charles called together those of his Council of War who were in Bristol to consider the Royalists' next move. Among those present was Edward Hyde (later Earl of Clarendon), as Chancellor an influential civilian member of the Council. He described later the situation as it appeared after the capture of Bristol:

> The King found it now high time to resolve to what action next to dispose his armies, and that their lying still so long there (for these agitations [the dispute between Rupert and Hertford] had kept the main work from going forward ten or twelve days, a time in that season unfortunately lost) had more weakened than refreshed them, having lost more men by storming the city than were afterwards by plundering it, those shoulders which had warmed themselves with the burden of pillage never quickly again submitting to the carriage of their arms.[1]

The foot regiments of the Oxford Army which had taken part in the assault on Bristol had been depleted by the same epidemic that had ravaged Essex's men and, even before the fighting, were noted as being very much under-strength:

> As Clarendon explained, the questions facing the Council of War were 'first, whether the armies should be united, and march in one upon the next design? And then, what that design should be?'[2]

There were a number of arguments against keeping the Oxford and Western Armies together. Although Bristol had fallen, much of the west of England, notably Exeter, Plymouth and large areas of Devon and Dorset, still remained in enemy hands. The Cornish forces had been badly depleted by their losses at Lansdown and Bristol, and were unwilling to go any further eastwards until Plymouth, which in enemy hands threatened their homes, had been reduced. Any attempt to compel them was likely to result in large-scale desertion, especially as their natural unruliness and indiscipline had been increased by the loss of so many of their officers. If they were allowed to operate nearer to home, there was reason to hope that many deserters would return to the colours and that the ranks could be filled out with new recruits. In any case, as Clarendon admitted: 'the truth is, their humours were not very gentle and agreeable, and apt to think that their prowess was not enough recompensed or valued.'[3] There would in any case be major logistical problems in keeping the Royalist armies together; resources were barely sufficient to maintain the 6,000 horse of the Oxford Army in one place for long. If the Western forces were sent initially to mop up Parliamentarian resistance in Dorset, this would not only ease the supply situation but also neatly solve the touchy protocol question of how best to cater for Prince Maurice, who would lose his command in a united army. So it was quickly agreed that the Earl of Carnarvon be sent at once, with his horse and dragoons, to operate around Dorchester, followed next day by Maurice, as new commander of the Western Army, with its foot and artillery.[4]

More difficult to resolve was the next move for the Oxford Army. Much debate has centred on the existence or otherwise of a grand Royalist strategy for the 1643 campaign. It has been postulated that the intention was for a three-pronged advance on London by the Earl of Newcastle's forces through the Eastern Association, the Western Army via the southern counties, and the Oxford Army retracing its march of 1642 along the Thames Valley, possibly with the ultimate objective of blockading the capital and starving it into surrender. There is in fact no firm evidence that such a strategy was ever formulated, and in any case its fulfilment would have met with virtually insuperable difficulties. We have seen already that the Western Royalist forces were neither willing nor able to advance much further eastwards until their home territories were secured, and similar considerations limited the options of the Earl of Newcastle. The Yorkshire contingent of his army, over whom he had only partial control, were unwilling to march any further south until Hull was reduced. This was, as Newcastle probably suspected from the outset, virtually impossible, with the Royalists faced by strong defences and an enemy kept constantly supplied, thanks to Parliamentarian supremacy at sea.

This left the Oxford Army. It had proved incapable of taking London in the autumn of 1642 and, though now more experienced, it was hardly stronger numerically, while the defences of the capital had unquestionably been greatly improved. Certainly for as long as Parliament's principal army under the Earl of Essex remained intact, the capture of London was probably beyond the capability of the King's main field army operating alone. Clarendon claimed that a number of military commanders favoured the London option, on the grounds that current Parliamentarian dissension there could be exploited, but he pointed out the serious problems facing the Royalists:

> ...in truth, it was a miserable army, lessened exceedingly by the losses it had sustained before Bristol; and when that part of it that was marched with prince Morice into the west, and which would not have marched any other way, the King had not much above six thousand foot to march with, though [if] he had left none at Bristol,... and that would have appeared a very small army to march towards London...[5]

So an alternative was sought after, and, as Clarendon explains, the Council's attention quickly became focused on the town of Gloucester.

The next resolution to be taken concerned the King's own motion with that army.

> There was not a man who did not think the reducing of Gloster, a city within little more than twenty miles of Bristol, of mighty importance to the King, if it might be done without a great expense of time and loss of men. It was the only garrison the rebels had between Bristol and Lancashire in the north part of England; and if it could be recovered, he would have the river of Severn entirely within his command, whereby his garrisons of Worcester and Shrewsbury and all those parts, might be supplied from Bristol, and the trade of that city thereby so advanced that the customs and duties might bring a notable revenue to the King, and the wealth of the city increasing, it might bear the greater burden for the war, a rich and populous county, which hitherto had rather yielded convenience of quarter than a settled contribution (that strong garrison [Gloucester] holding not only the whole forest [of Dean] division, which is a fourth part of the county of Gloster, absolutely in obedience, but so alarmed all the other parts thereof that none of the gentry, who for the most part were well affected, durst stay at their own houses), might be wholly the King's quarter, and by how much it had offended and disquieted the King more than other counties, by so much the more money might be raised upon them besides the general weekly contributions, the yeomanry, who had been most forward and seditious, being very wealthy, but able to redeem their delinquency at a high price. And these arguments were fully pressed by the well-affected gentry of the county, who had carried themselves honestly, and suffered very much by doing so, and undertook great levies of men if this work were first done. There was another argument of no less, if not greater, moment than all the rest: if Gloster were reduced, there would be need no forces to be left in Wales, and all those soldiers might then be drawn to the marching army, and the contributions and other taxes assigned to the payment of it. Indeed the King would have a glorious and entire part of his kingdom to have contended with the rest.[6]

Not everyone in the Royalist camp was happy with the decision. Lord Spencer, who may have commanded the artillery during the siege, told his wife on 9 August, 'at sunset', that:

...the King's sudden resolution of going before Gloucester hath extremely disappointed me...The King's going to Gloucester is in the opinion of most very unadvised. I find the Queen is unsatisfied with it; so is all the people of quality.[7]

The main disadvantage for the Royalists would arise if faced with prolonged and determined resistance by the defenders of Gloucester, which would afford a breathing space for the Parliamentarian cause as a whole to recover. With this in mind, the supposed attitude of the Governor of Gloucester, Colonel Edward Massey, played a key part in Royalist decision-making.

Born *c.* 1618 in Cheshire, Massey, described by Clarendon as 'a wonderful vain and weak man, but very busy and undertaking',[8] had been a professional soldier and military engineer before the war, serving on the Continent and in the Scots Wars. He seems to have had a similarly fundamentally self-interested attitude towards the outbreak of civil war, as did many other career soldiers, and in the summer of 1642 he initially considered enlisting with the forces which the King was raising at York, before concluding that he had better opportunities for promotion with the Parliamentarians (though he claimed his motive to have been an unwillingness to serve with the Roman Catholics whom Charles was recruiting). Appointed in 1642 as Lieutenant-Colonel in the Earl of Stamford's Regiment of Foot, early in the following year Massey was made Governor of Gloucester.

Even before the fall of Bristol, the Royalists had been pondering the best means of taking Gloucester. On 17 July, one of Rupert's officers, Lord Grandison, wrote to the Prince:

> Sir, I did forget to tell your Highness that the best way to enter the town of Gloucester will be by putting some of the garrison of Worcester into boats, to fall down the river to that side of Gloucester which lieth most open, and will be very easy to them to master, while we assault on this side, and Vavasour, with his force, come off the forest side from Hereford.[9]

By early August the Royalists were apparently confident that Massey was willing to surrender Gloucester, provided that certain conditions were met. Clandestine contacts seem to have taken place over several days, the Royalist intermediary being Major William Legge, a close confidant of Rupert who, as a fellow professional soldier, may well have served previously with Massey. On 7 August the Royalist Major-General of Dragoons, Sir Arthur Aston, wrote to Rupert from Painswick to inform him, accurately as it transpired, that:

> From Major Legge you will understand the resolution of the Governor of Gloucester, whereupon I conceive that the summoning of him to surrender the city will be to little purpose, as yet, until we can put him to some distress.[10]

However on the following day the King's Secretary of State, Sir Edward Nicholas, wrote confidently to Charles:

> This gentleman, Captain Presland Molyneux, hath this day been with the Lords here, and told them that he is an ancient and intimate acquaintance of Captain Massey... that he knows Massey's affections are to serve your Majesty, and that he had put himself into your service, but that he was refused the employment he desired... This Captain Molyneux doubts not, but if he may be permitted to go to Massey, he shall persuade him to render himself and Gloucester into your Majesty's hands...[11]

Just how much substance there was to this is hard now to discover. It may be that Massey was, as suggested, simply playing for time, or he may indeed have been considering turning his coat provided he could receive satisfactory assurances. According to Clarendon, whose account may well be substantially accurate, Massey had told Legge that:

> ...if the king himself came with his army, and summoned it [Gloucester] he would not hold it against him, for it would not stand with his conscience to fight against the person of the king – besides that in such a case he should be able to persuade those of the town, which otherwise he could not do.[12]

In reality Massey was in a difficult situation and perhaps mainly concerned to reach the best solution for his own interests, but certainly the expectation of his defection was a major consideration in the Royalist Council of War's decision on 4 August to make Gloucester their next objective.

For the Parliamentarians, the loss of Bristol was the climax of a spring and summer of increasing discontent and despondency. After an auspicious beginning with the capture of Reading (27 April) Essex's campaign in the Thames Valley had foundered as his men were stricken by what was apparently an epidemic of typhus, brought on by their unhealthy living conditions in the low-lying country around Thame. Essex was always sensitive to criticism and slights, whether real or imagined, and the stagnation of his operations against Oxford brought him a steadily rising influx of both. His immediate reaction, not for the last time in his career, was to threaten resignation, which would have been a serious political embarrassment to the war party in Westminster headed by John Pym.

However Essex's performance over the next few weeks did little to boost confidence in him. He was consistently outmatched by Rupert's cavalry, who raided as far as High Wycombe, close enough to the capital to cause considerable alarm. Since the spring the Oxford Army had been awaiting the arrival from the north of England of a huge convoy of munitions which had landed at Bridlington with Queen Henrietta Maria in February. Only when it arrived would the King's main army be sufficiently well equipped to take the field, and so its fate was of vital concern to both sides. On 3 July the Queen, with a great train of 150 wagons, left Newark on Trent on the most perilous phase of her journey to Oxford.

Essex failed either to intercept the convoy or to engage the escort which Rupert was taking to meet the Queen. Not surprisingly, this aroused further criticism, to which the Earl responded by blaming his weakness in cavalry, and on 9 July proposed in the House of Lords that peace feelers be put out to the King, adding that if these were rejected Charles should be requested to retire from the field while the two armies settled the issue in a trial by battle![13] The idea was universally rejected, and instead (as may have been Essex's real intention) it was agreed that his army should be reinforced by an additional 500 horse.

On 11 July Rupert linked up with the Queen at Stratford-upon-Avon and three days later, to the sound of pealing bells in a city already rejoicing at news of the victory at Roundway Down, the combined force, with its great train of munitions, including a number of pieces of artillery, entered Oxford.

Pym's immediate reaction was to call for 6,500 more horse to be raised for Essex's army, but Parliamentarian morale soon slumped still further on news of the loss of Bristol. To the people of London, already partially starved of supplies by the King's outposts to the west of the capital, and alarmed by a brief Royalist uprising in Kent, this latest disaster seemed further evidence of the failings of the Earl of Essex. A new wave of criticism followed, with Essex caricatured sprawling at his ease with a glass of wine in one hand and tobacco pipe in the other. The Earl's anger was intensified when it was announced that a new army which the City of London was financing was earmarked to be given to Sir William Waller, despite his recent defeat.

Waller was indeed high in the favour of the war party in Parliament, and the enmity between him and Essex was heightened when Sir William blamed his defeat at Roundway Down on lack of support from the Earl. With the Parliamentarian cause seemingly in danger of breaking down because of the dissension in its leadership, the peace faction in the House of Lords, headed by the Earl of Holland, suggested peace proposals which, by giving the King control of the militia, surrendering all fortresses to him and allowing expelled pro-Royalist members of Parliament to resume their seats, would virtually have handed him victory.[14] Holland and his supporters hoped for backing from the disgruntled Essex, but the latter declined to declare himself openly in their favour. The Earl and his officers continued to press the claims of their own army, on 28 July telling Parliament that it now had only 2,500 horse and 3,000 foot fit to fight. Essex urged that the proposed new recruits and additional money and supplies should be used to rebuild his army, rather than to form a new one, and that Essex himself, as Lord General, should have the sole right to grant commissions. In a sideswipe at Waller, the Earl also demanded an investigation into the causes of the defeats in the west.

In order to ensure his support, Pym and his supporters granted all of Essex's requests except for an enquiry. During the opening days of August Pym worked frantically to hold together the wavering Parliamentarian cause. He was the moving spirit behind the measures to restore confidence in Essex, and on 2 August he set up a small Council of War, whose members included members of Parliament and some merchants and soldiers, in order to give a tighter direction to the running of the Parliamentarian war effort.

Gradually Pym regained some measure of control. On 7 August, amid demonstrations by both pro- and anti-war supporters, Holland's peace proposals were narrowly voted down.

Nevertheless, the overall situation remained grim. The only gleam of hope on the military horizon was Cromwell's fairly minor victory on 28 July over Royalist cavalry led by Charles Cavendish at Gainsborough. But this on its own was insufficient to alter the military picture, either locally or as a whole. With Parliament seemingly forced back firmly on to a defensive strategy, Pym began to seek means to tilt the balance through an alliance with the Scots. But in the short term the dominant question remained whether the Parliamentarian cause could survive long enough for Scottish aid to arrive. The outcome of events at Gloucester might well be decisive in answering this.

2

The Siege of Gloucester
August–September 1643

In 1643 Gloucester had a population of about 5,000. Like many other English towns at the time, the older part of the city was still surrounded by its medieval walls, although suburbs had extended beyond them to the north, east and south. On its western side Gloucester was protected by the River Severn. As well as being a small port, Gloucester was chiefly engaged in clothing manufacture, together with a few smaller trades. Gloucester's geographical location meant that it controlled the route northwards along the Severn to Worcester and Shrewsbury, and also communications from London and Oxford to South Wales.

The population of the town included a strong Puritan element, and this had helped ensure Gloucester's support for Parliament from the early days of the war. There were however a number of Royalist sympathisers within the town, while most of the neighbouring gentry also favoured the King. The bulk of the town council were of the Puritan persuasion, and even before the formal outbreak of war they had begun work on strengthening Gloucester's defences. Early in 1643 Edward Massey was appointed Governor, and Gloucester soon found itself involved in active military operations. The capture of Cirencester by Prince Rupert in February 1643 brought the war much closer to the city, and a month later the Royalists made their first attempt to take Gloucester. A force of 2,000 men, hastily recruited in South Wales by Lord Herbert and known as the 'mushroom army' because of its rapid formation and equally speedy destruction, was defeated by Sir William Waller just across the River Severn from Gloucester at Highnam.

Although the immediate threat was for the moment reduced, the Gloucester Parliamentarians reacted in April by raising the 'Town Regiment', probably based around the existing Trained Band, and pressed on with work on strengthening the defences. After all, as a Parliamentarian writer admitted, Gloucester was 'open on three sides at least, and had no considerable defence'.[1]

This was by no means the only problem facing Massey in the summer of 1643. He had an uneasy relationship with the local Parliamentarian leadership, headed by Alderman Pury, who possibly disapproved of Massey's rather questionable loyalties at the start of the war, exacerbated by the Governor's own somewhat prickly personality. Lack of pay made the loyalty of some of the garrison troops uncertain, and, although Massey appears to have put a brave face on matters and 'appeared in publicke, rode from place to place with a cheerful aspect',[2] privately he was considerably more doubtful regarding his prospects of success. In late July, following the loss of Bristol, he wrote to the Speaker of the House of Commons:

> Our wants are so great, and this city so averse to us, that our power cannot enforce men beyond their wills, which I had done, and would do, if our regiment [part of the Earl of Stamford's Foot] might have equalled the city in strength; but now, what with the general discontent, of both of the city soldiers and our own, we stand at present as betrayed unless speedily your care prevent it. Alderman Pury and some few of the citizens, I dare say, are still cordial to us, but I fear ten for one induce the other way. If your supply come speedily, you may have hopes to call Gloucester still yours; if not, I have lost mine, for alone ourselves we cannot act.[3]

Massey, who certainly exaggerated the degree of Royalist support in the town, gives the impression of having virtually lost hope, and it was probably at this time that he was putting out feelers to the Royalists. However for some reason, we cannot be sure exactly why, his attitude changed over the next few days, and by the time that the enemy approached Gloucester on 6 August both Massey and the great majority of the townsfolk were set upon resisting.

The army which King Charles led against Gloucester was numerically probably the largest he ever commanded in the entire war. As well as about 12,000 men of the Oxford Army, including the nine regiments of foot which Rupert had taken to Bristol and 1,000 'commanded' musketeers drawn from the units left there for the moment, the King was reinforced by almost 5,000 men raised in South Wales by Lord Herbert and commanded by Sir William Vavasour, by detachments from Bristol, Oxford and the Welsh border, and by various small contingents brought in by local Royalist gentry. Cavalier strength may have approached 20,000[4], although many of these troops were of poor quality and low morale, and supplying such large numbers would present major difficulties.

By 10 August Gloucester was entirely surrounded, and the King, establishing his headquarters at Matson House, 2½ miles south-west of the town, sent in a summons to surrender, promising free pardon to all.

He was probably confident that Massey would comply, after perhaps negotiating some face-saving formula. However the brief response was one of defiance, carried, in Clarendon's scornful description, by:

> ...two citizens from the town, with lean, sharp, and bald visages, indeed faces so strange and unusual, and in such a garb and posture, that at once made the most severe countenance merry, and the most cheerful heart sad, for it was impossible such ambassadors could bring less than defiance.[5]

Royalist hopes of Gloucester's bloodless capitulation were dashed, but their Council of War resolved to open siege operations. The King and his commanders were partly influenced by considerations of prestige, for to march tamely away from Gloucester would be portrayed by the enemy, with some justification, as a major Royalist reverse. They had also received reports that provisions were low in the town, its defences poor, and that there was a strong pro-Royalist faction among the townsfolk who might provide a 'fifth column' within. Even if Parliament were able to put together a relief force, the Royalists might hope to bring it to battle in an advantageous situation:

> Above all, the confidence of the soldiers of the best experience moved his majesty, who, upon riding about the town and taking a near view of it, were clear of opinion that they should be able in less than ten days by approach to win it.[6]

This view apparently conflicted with that of Prince Rupert, who reportedly wanted to storm Gloucester in the same way that he had Bristol. This option was rejected by the King and his Council of War, probably because of the fear of high casualties, which would cripple them for the remainder of the campaigning season. Clarendon suggests that this decision met with Rupert's strong disagreement, and that he declined to command the siege operations, though he apparently did not take his opposition to the point of voting against the plan in the Council of War, 'that he might not be thought accountable for any accidents which should attend that service', and would confine his attentions to the cavalry.[7] It is unclear how much credence should be placed on this. The regular siege operations would be directed by Patrick Ruthven, Earl of Forth, the vastly experienced Scottish professional soldier who was Lord General, and effectively senior commander, of the Oxford Army. It was a responsibility which would normally have been his in any case.

The defenders of Gloucester totalled about 1,500 men including part of the Earl of Stamford's Regiment and the Town Regiment of 500 men, together with a troop of horse and some dragoons under another Scots professional soldier, Colonel Arthur Forbes. To these were added some local auxiliaries and remnants of units which had been at Bristol. Contrary to Royalist belief, the garrison was reasonably well supplied and equipped, although it had only forty barrels of powder, which were supplemented by three barrels a week manufactured in the town.

However, Gloucester's defences, despite the work which had been carried out at intervals since before the start of the war, were still incomplete. The west side of the town was unprotected, apart from the not inconsiderable barrier of the River Severn. The medieval walls only survived intact between the South Gate and the north-eastern corner of the town. The gap running along the northern edge of Gloucester was filled by earth defences. These, built according to the Dutch pattern, were commonly employed in fortifications during the Civil War, and might have been quite elaborate and formidable. The evidence suggests however that they may have been relatively weak at Gloucester during the summer of 1643, and that they concentrated mainly on protecting the entrances to the town. In other sectors they may have been little more than a series of unconnected earth forts or 'sconces'. The defences were particularly weak on the eastern and south-eastern sides of the town, where the Royalists were able to mount gun batteries 'within pistol shot'.

It was probably for this reason that when the Cavalier bombardment began on 13 August, it was concentrated on the south-east angle of the defences and quickly opened up a breach. However the defenders were able to fill this with wool sacks and gabions (large baskets) filled with earth. Five days later the Royalist guns renewed their assault, firing over 150 'great shot', which 'shrewdly battered the wall, but our earth workes stood firm'.[8]

Keeping the besiegers supplied with munitions was a major undertaking for the Royalist Ordnance Office in Oxford. On 3 August, in preparation for the attack on Gloucester, the General of the Ordnance, Henry, Lord Percy, had issued orders for the preparation of a large munitions train to accompany the foot which the Lord General was taking from Oxford to join the King. It included over twenty wagons, carrying a mortar piece, and about 260 iron roundshot for demi-cannon, culverin and twelve-pounder guns, as well as hand 'granadoes', firepikes and a large variety of other supplies and equipment.[9]

The demands of the siege put a heavy strain on the still fairly limited resources of the Royalist Ordnance Office. Supplies were sent constantly to the King's forces at Gloucester, and included ammunition and equipment for the infantry. On 14 August a new mortar piece was despatched to replace that sent in the original convoy, which was 'broken', as well as a steady supply of powder and shot. Siege artillery consumed enormous quantities of gunpowder, and by the middle of August there were signs that Oxford's gunpowder-makers were having difficulty in keeping up with demand. On 14 August only five hundredweight of powder could be sent in response to a request for fifty hundredweight.[10]

Henry, Lord Percy, the General of the Ordinance, was not regarded as particularly efficient, but his Lieutenant-General, Sir John Heydon, was a highly competent officer who had occupied the same post prior to the war, and he was usually able to meet the bulk of demands. Supplies were conveyed in wagons, organised by the Wagon-Master-General, who either used transport from the army's own stock or hired or commandeered wagons with civilian drivers. The Royalists were fortunate in that their lines of communication with Oxford were short, and also reasonably secure from enemy attack.

Meanwhile at Gloucester the defenders responded to the Royalist bombardment by hastily erecting an inner line of defences between the threatened South and East Gates, demolishing some houses in order to give a clear field of fire. The defences on the western side of the town were provided mainly by the Severn and by flooding some marshes, and were never seriously tested by Vavasour's poorly motivated and equipped Welsh troops, who faced that sector.

Most of the labour involved in the constant strengthening and repair of Gloucester's defences was provided by civilians, including women and children. Even with the bulk of the troops thus released for combat duty, there were not enough soldiers to man all the defences adequately, so they were concentrated at what were deemed to be the most vulnerable points, with reserves of 120 men held at the Wheat Market in Southgate Street and at the main magazine in St Mary de Crypt Church.

The Parliamentarians were assisted by an apparent lack of vigour in the Royalist conduct of the siege. The King's officers, including experienced soldiers such as Sir Jacob Astley, Major-General of Foot, and Will Legge, had assured Charles that Gloucester could be reduced within ten days, and the Royalists proved ill-prepared for prolonged siege operations. Clarendon later admitted that the King had 'neither money, men, or materials requisite for a siege'[11], while the Queen, now back in Oxford and reluctant to release the munitions which she had brought with such difficulty from Holland, was said to be angry at what she saw as a waste of resources.

The result was a lack of consistency and clear strategy in the Royalist operations. After failing in an attempt to cut off Gloucester's water supply, the Cavaliers evidently decided to adopt a low-cost approach of attrition and bombardment, aimed at weakening the defences and defenders sufficiently to allow an assault without incurring high casualties. The disadvantage with such tactics was that they were likely to be both prolonged and uncertain in outcome, but the Royalist command seem at first to have discounted the likelihood of any speedy Parliamentarian relief attempt.

The initial bombardment was therefore concentrated against the south-east angle of Gloucester's defences, where the ground was higher and would, if captured, allow the besiegers to dominate the remainder of the town. The intention was to combine an artillery bombardment with mining operations designed to create a breach at the East Gate, and then to launch major assaults here and at the south-east angle. Civilian miners were conscripted from the Forest of Dean, but not surprisingly lacked enthusiasm for the task. On about 20 August the Sheriff of Gloucestershire, Baynham Throckmorton, harassed and embarrassed, complained to Lord Percy:

> Last night the miners were here and this morninge most of them are gone home without ever acquaintinge me with it (notwithstanding my strict commands to them to ye contrary) some are here, but of the most ignorant of them; And therefore I doe forebeare to send them to your Lordship: I have already now sent away servants of my owne with strict warrants and commands to bringe them and more with them presently hither, and have sent strict orders both to some Horse and Foote that I have in that Countrey, to bringe them away by force, and not neglect a minute of an houre in it day and night: And I am confident that by tomorrow noone here will be some reasonable number of them, and they shall instantly be brought to your lordship: I beseech you, my Lord, judge charitably of this unhappy incident, for never man had such rogues to deal with, but I have given order to my officers, to burne ye houses of those that resist or refuse instantly to come with them...[12]

Not only were problems encountered with the recalcitrant miners, but the artillery bombardment was also proving ineffective. As well as ordinary artillery fire, attempts were made to fire houses with red-hot shot and 'granadoes' fired by the mortar. This again failed to achieve the desired result, partly because of frequent interruptions caused by shortage of ammunition and partly because the fuses fitted to the mortar shells were often too long, meaning that they either buried themselves in the ground and exploded harmlessly, or were extinguished before they could detonate. A Parliamentarian account described how one shell 'fell into the street near the South gate, but a woman coming by with a payle of water, threw the water thereon, and extinguished the fuse thereof, so that it did not break.'¹³ Further delays resulted when the Royalist mortar, said to be the biggest in England, exploded.

In preparation for an eventual assault, the Royalist troops spent much of the siege engaged in the unpleasant and frequently dangerous task of digging trenches and zigzag approaches to Gloucester's defences. To encourage them in the work, many senior officers took their turn in the trenches, among them Prince Rupert, who had two narrow escapes – the first from an exploding hand grenade and the second when his helmet was hit by a stone hurled by the defenders. By 2 September the Royalists were within pistol shot of the defences, but Massey, who throughout the siege mounted an active and aggressive defence, early in the morning brought up a light gun, loaded with case shot, into a concealed position within the defences. Opening fire, the gun shattered the wooden mantle erected to protect the Royalist sappers, allowing Parliamentarian musketeers and 'granadoe-men' to pour a heavy fire into the enemy, driving them back.

When the reluctant Forest of Dean miners were eventually rounded up, they seem to have made at least three mining attempts during the course of the siege. These proved entirely ineffective, in part because of the waterlogged condition of much of the ground, but also because of lack of coordination between the different attempts. According to the Royalist officer, Captain John Gwynne, who was present: 'had there been as much care taken in making one mine ready, as in the making of the other two which stayed for it, probably we had carried the town.'¹⁴

Royalist attacks were also hindered by the many ditches around the city. Among the victims of the terrain was an ingenious device suggested by the Royalist scholar and divine, Dr John Chillingworth. He devised a type of siege engine, evidently inspired by those of classical times, and a number were constructed at Lord Forth's encampment at Llanthony. According to the Parliamentarian writer John Corbet, who probably saw them:

> They framed great store of these unperfect and troublesome engines to assault the lower parts of the city. Those engines ran upon wheels, with planks musket-proof placed on the axel-tree, with holes for musket-shot and a bridge before it, the end whereof (the wheels falling into the ditch) was to rest upon our breastworks.¹⁵

It seems unlikely that these machines were ever put to the test, for they were afterwards found abandoned in a nearby marsh. It has been suggested however that their legacy remains in the shape of a well-known nursery rhyme:

> Humpty Dumpty fell in a beck,
> With all his sinews about his neck,
> All the King's surgeons and all the King's knights,
> Couldn't put Humpty Dumpty to rights.[16]

On 25 August Lord Spencer felt confident enough to tell his wife:

> Our gallery will be finished within this day or two, and then we shall soon despatch our mine, and them with it. Many of the soldiers are confident that we shall have the town within this four day, which I extremely long for, not that I am weary of the siege; for really, though we suffer many inconveniences, yet I am not ill-pleased at this variety, so directly opposite to one another, as the being in the trenches with so much good company, together with the noise and tinta-marre of guns and drums, the horrid spectacles and hideous cries of dead and hurt men, is the solitariness of my quarter.[17]

Massey did what he could to hinder Royalist progress by means of vigorously mounted sorties, and by keeping up a steady fire on targets of opportunity with the fifteen guns belonging to the garrison. The Parliamentarians were particularly active in night raids, mainly carried out by the men of Stamford's Regiment. John Corbet admitted:

> Our men from the walls could doe little to retard their pioneers, but by severall sallies with small parties fell into their trenches, beate them out, gained some working tooles, arms and prisoners, and retreated without losse.[18]

Not all raids were as successful, however. After a night raid on 16 August on the Royalist quarters at Llananthony, the Cavaliers reported finding twenty-four 'bluecoats' dead in one trench. Two days later, in the largest operation mounted by the garrison, Major Pudsey and Captain Cray, with 400 musketeers, attacked the Royalist battery at Kingsholm. They succeeded in nailing up one gun before being driven back by Royalist reinforcements. In a sortie in the early hours of 3 September, five men, led by John Barnewood, a manufacturer of granadoes, slipped out of a sally port near the East Gate and crept up to one of the sites of the Royalist mining operations:

> After he had taken aside the board that covered it, and a pretty while viewed them, [he] fired and cast a granadoe in among them, our foure musketters playing at them as they ran out of it, and so retreated without harme. We killed foure and hurt others.[19]

By the beginning of September fighting had grown more intense, as the Royalists worked their way in closer, and a major assault on the vulnerable south-east angle of the town seemed likely within a few days. In an effort to weaken the morale of the defenders, on 3 September the Cavaliers fired arrows into Gloucester, bearing papers with the message:

> These are to let you understand your god Waller hath forsaken you, and hath retired himselfe to the Tower of London. Essex is beaten like a dog: yielde to the King's mercie in time, otherwise, if we enter perforce, no quarter, for such obstinate traiterly rogues.

The defenders replied with a defiant verse:

> Waller's no god of ours, base rogues, you lie,
> Our God survives from all eternitie;
> Though Essex beaten be, as you doe say,
> Rome's yoke we are resolv'd nere to obey;
> But for our cabbages which ye have eaten
> Be sure ere long ye shall be soundly beaten.
> Quarter we ask you none; if we fall downe,
> King Charles will lose true subjects with the towne.[20]

But for all their bold words of defiance the defenders were growing desperate. They had no certain word of any relief attempt, and Royalist pressure was mounting. Unless help came in time, Gloucester was likely to fall within a week.

When news reached London that Gloucester was under attack, its fate overrode all other considerations. The Parliamentarian leadership were keenly aware that the loss of the town might sound the death knell of their hopes, while the citizens of London were aware that if Gloucester fell they were likely to be the next target of the victorious Cavaliers. The only force available to go to the relief of Gloucester was the under-strength army of the Earl of Essex, and, abandoning for the moment their plans to form a new army under Waller, Parliament made strengthening Essex a priority. Orders were issued for 2,000 men to be conscripted to fill some of the gaps in his ranks, while five regiments of the London Trained Band, among the best of the English militia units, with one regiment of the city horse, together with Randell Mainwaring's Regiment of Foot from the London garrison, were to reinforce Essex.[21] The citizens of London were subjected to a forced subsidy to provide funds and, in an effort to encourage recruiting, shops were closed to allow their workforce to enlist, exhorted by the urgings of preachers at the street corners.

Just how successful these attempts were was debatable; the Royalist propaganda sheet *Mercurius Aulicus* claimed that many of the new levies deserted on their way to join Essex, a number being found drowned in the Thames.[22] These suggestions of a certain lack of enthusiasm were partly confirmed by Henry Foster, a sergeant the Red Regiment of the London Trained Band, who later reported in his journal of the march that after a stirring send-off by the citizens of the capital on 23 August:

> Our red Regiment of the Train'd Bands marched into the new Artillery ground, and from thence that night we marched to Brainford [Brentford], and came thither about one a clocke in the morning; from whence the next day many of our Citizens who seemed very forward and willing at the first to march with us, yet upon some pretences and faire excuses returned home againe hiring others to go in their roome others returned home againe the same night before they came to Brainford.[23]

The Earl of Essex, however, faced with the greatest challenge of his military career and at last — or so it probably seemed to him — recognised as indispensable, appeared to have thrown off all of his doubts and discontents. After reviewing on 24 August the 6,000 men, 3,500 foot and 2,500 horse with 'a brave train of Artillery' initially under his command on Hounslow Heath, Essex sent a message to Parliament, proclaiming:

> I am tomorrow, god willing, beginning my march, and if the army be as willing to march as I shall be to lead them and the town should wait until we can relieve them, I shall endeavour it, or perish in the attempt.[24]

Travelling via Colnbrook (where he issued his men with a fortnight's pay), Beaconsfield and Aylesbury, Essex marched to Brackley Heath to await the arrival of the London Brigade, formed from the Trained Bands, together with various stragglers and conscripted recruits for Essex's army.

Henry Foster and his Trained Band comrades had had a reasonably easy introduction to the realities of campaign life, the novelty so far offsetting the inevitable discomforts, although the soldiers were somewhat shaken on 25 August, after they bivouacked for the night at Chalfont St Giles, when 'a souldier belonging to Liutenant-Colonell [William] Tompson was accidentally slaine by shooting off a musket by one of his fellow Souldiers though at a great distance from him, yet shot him in the head whereof he died.'[25]

On 27 August Foster's regiment again found reasonably satisfactory quarters at 'Mr Cheyney's House' at Chesham, where, most importantly so far as the soldiers were concerned, 'we were well accommodated for Beere having great plenty, two or theee hundred this night lay in one Barne.'[26] But by 31 August a hint of disillusionment was creeping into Foster's voice. When the 5,000 men of the London Brigade halted for the night at Stratton Audley, he noted, in what would be a recurrent theme: 'here was little provision either for Officers or souldiers.'[27]

However any fall in morale was largely forgotten next day, when the Londoners rendezvoused with Essex and his troops at Bayards Green, 3 miles from Brackley, where:

> ...our Brigade met my Lord Generall with his whole Army, whereat was great shouting and Triumph as he passed by to take a view of our Regiments, the whole Army being drawne up in their severall Regiments, continued there about an houre and then we marched away: It was a goodly and glorious sight to see the whole Army of Horse and Foot together, it is conceived by those that viewed our Army well that wee did consist of (to speake of the least) 15,000 horse and foot, some speak of many more.

Even though these estimates were probably slightly high and, as was now becoming usual, that night 'we were very much scanted of Victualls'[28], Foster and his comrades remained confident.

Essex's own troops were probably cheered by an issue of new clothing, including 3,336 coats, mostly red or grey, 4,260 pairs of shoes and 2,870 'snapsacks'. Essex was also joined at Brackley by the Midlands cavalry regiments of Thomas, Lord Grey of Groby and Lord Denbigh, together with three independent troops of horse under Sir Samuel Luke.

The Royalists had professed confidence that Essex would never reach Gloucester, claiming that his army would be halted or even destroyed by the superior Royalist cavalry, particularly as he entered the open terrain of the Cotswolds. Skirmishing had indeed begun even before the London Brigade joined Essex. On 26 August some of the Parliamentarian horse under Sir Philip Stapleton had a brief engagement with Royalist cavalry, who probably came from Banbury. A more serious encounter came on 2 September, at Deddington. On the previous evening, following the army review, a Scottish professional soldier, Colonel John Middleton, had been ordered to quarter in the village and:

> ...hearing there of two Regiments of the Enemie's horse, sent Captain Middleton with two companies of Dragoons, and Captain Hale with a

party of horse to approach the town: but the Enemy retreated to a passage toward Oxford, where the Lord Wilmot [Lieutenant-General of Horse in the Oxford Army] was with 50 troops more. Our Scouts followed so far that they encountered with the other Scouts, and fired at each other. Next morning Col. Middleton only with his own Regiment, and Sir James Ramsey's, advanced to the Passe, where the Enemy stood in two great bodies, and after some skirmish got the Passe, placing Dragooners to maintain it, and when the Enemy drew up again towards it, he received them with such resolution that the skirmish (notwithstanding the inequality of forces) was maintained till 3 a clock in the afternoon; they then retreating. Col. Middleton by his Excellencie's command marched toward the Army; which the Enemy perceiving, sent out a party of horse to fall on his Rere, who followed them through Deddington, which Col. Middleton perceiving, commanded the Scottish Reformado officers to receive them; which they accordingly did, and beat them back through the town in great confusion. The Enemies' losse in this skirmish was greater than ours, though not many lost on either side.[29]

The same evening, near Adderbury, Essex's Lifeguard and Regiment of Horse, together with that commanded by Lord Grey, routed a small party of horse from Banbury.

By 3 September the Parliamentarians had reached Chipping Norton on the fringes of the Cotswolds. Though Wilmot's horse continued to shadow them, no serious attack was launched. It may well be that Wilmot, a generally capable commander, had insufficient strength to bring on a serious engagement, and was intended only to wear down and tire the Parliamentarians, who, with the arrival of the main force of Royalist cavalry led by Prince Rupert, were about to meet a sterner challenge.

The rolling open downland around Stow-on-the-Wold presented the Royalists with their best opportunity to bring their cavalry to bear and here, on 4 September, Prince Rupert made his major effort to halt or seriously damage the relief force. As usual, the accounts of the opposing sides differ widely, but a fairly clear picture of events emerges. On the night of 3 September the London Brigade, which that day had formed the vanguard of Essex's army, was quartered around the village of Addington, about a mile to the east of Stow:

> ...our red Regiment of the Trained Band was constrained to march halfe a mile further to get quarter, we were now in the Van of the whole Army, having not so much as one Troope of Horse quartered near us, but we were no sooner in our quarters, and set down our Armes, intending a little to refresh ourselves, but presently there was an Alarme beat up; and wee being

the frontier Regiment nearest the enemy, were presently all drawn into a Body, and stood upon our Guard all that night, we were in great distraction, having not any horse to send out as Scouts, to give us any Intelligence: my Lord General with his Army lay at Chipping Norton about three miles behind us; who had an Alarm there given by the enemy the same night also. Our regiment stood in the open field all night, having neither bread nor water to refresh ourselves, having also marched the day before without any sustenance nor durst kindle any fire though it was a very cold night.[30]

Dawn on 4 September brought further bad news for the cold and hungry Londoners:

...we got some refreshment for our soldiers, which was no sooner done, but news was brought us, that the Enemy was within halfe a mile of the Town, which proved to be true, for presently one rid downe to us having his horse shot in the neck all bloody, and told us the enemy was at the townes end; also one Trooper slaine a quarter of a mile above the town, one of our soldiers stript him, and brought his clothes to us. It was a little open Village, the enemy might have come in upon us every way; therefore we conceiving it not safe to abide in the town, drew up our Regiment presently into a body, and marched into a broad open field to the top of the hill; the blew Regiment of the train'd Bands was quartered within lesse than halfe a mile of us, but came not up to us. Being come into the field we saw about 4 or 5,000 of the enemie's horse surrounding of us, one rid post to my Lord Generall to inform him of it. One great body of their horse stood facing us upon the top of the hill at our townes end, within lesse than a quarter of a mile from us; another great body of their horse was in the valley, upon our right flank as we stood, and a third great squadron of their horse were going up to the top of a hill, in the reere of us; by all which it appears, they had an intent to have surrounded our City Regiments, and to have cut us off; we stood and faced one another for the space of halfe an houre, then 6 or 7 of our men who had horses, rod up to them, and came within lesse than musket shot, flourishing their swords, daring them, and one or two of our men fired upon their forlorn hope. We had lined the hedges with musketeers, which they perceiving did not move towards our body, but only stood and faced us. Then some of the Auxiliary forces came up to us, at whose coming we gave a great shout, and then by and by after we sawe my Lord General's forces coming down the hill about a mile and a halfe behind us...[31]

Another Parliamentarian account takes up the story from the viewpoint of Essex's men:

Collonell Harvey with his Regiment of horse, and two regiments of foot, advanced a little before toward the Right hand, and the City Regiments upon the left, under the conduct of Lieutenant Colonell Bayley, Generall Adjutant of the foot: and resolutely faced Prince Rupert on both sides, who then appeared, with above four thousand horse, drawne upon the hills: and in the bottome on this side Stoe the old, when Prince Rupert sent a strong party of horse to encompasse Colonell Harvey, Sir James Ramsey having the Vanne of the Army, and apprehending Colonell Harvey's danger, approached to his relief with his own, Colonell Middleton's and Colonell Sheffield's Regiments; made the Enemy speedily and confusedly retreat to their body, and pursued them to a hedge, where not above two could passé on breast: our forlorne Hope commanded by Captain Carre, who had a little before passed the hedge ere we could come to second them, were charged by Urrey [Sir John Urry, Sergeant Major General of Horse to Prince Rupert] with four times their number, and received them with much gallantrye, yet charged not through them in respect of the Enemies' Reserves, but made purposely a retreat towards the hedge, where we had an ambuscade of Musquetiers. The rest of the Regiments were by this time passed the hedge, and made the Enemies speedily retreat to their main Body.[32]

It is interesting to compare the Royalist account of the same incident:

Yesterday Colonel Sir John Urrey and Sergeant Major [John] Marrow (being appointed by Prince Rupert to charge the Rebels forlorne hope, with a part of the Queen's Regiment) went on so resolutely, and were so well followed by their commanded men, that the Rebels presently fell to their old discipline of running away. At first the Rebels discharged three or four Canons from an advantageous hill, having lined two sides of a corner hedge with Dragoons, who from both sides gave the King's Forces a Salue of Muskets as they advanced to charge their horse party but by that time the Rebels had discharged their Carbines and Pistols, these Troopes of Her Majestie's Regiment fell in with their swords, and chaced the Rebels (according to the custome) till they came to the maine body of their Army, which then lay shelter'd in a place that was inaccessible. There were killed of the Rebels 14 or 15 in the place, some prisoners taken and one of their leaders wounded. The King's Forces lost not a man, onely one horse was shot.[33]

Whatever the exact sequence of events, it is clear that only a minor action had taken place, and Rupert had possibly lost an opportunity to inflict a sharp defeat on the London Brigade while it was unsupported. Foster certainly felt so, commenting:

> ...their intent was to have compassed us on every side, but the Lord prevented them, they might have spoiled our whole Regiment, had they in the morning come down upon us when we were taking a little food to refresh ourselves, the enemy being then but half a mile off.[34]

However a body of foot, given time to form into defensive formation, could be a very tough nut to crack, and the Prince may have considered an attack too risky.

He would get no other real opportunity that day. The Royalists gradually pulled back into and beyond Stow, evidently watching for any enemy weakness or disarray which they could exploit, while the Parliamentarians, in close order, headed by Sir Philip Stapleton with Essex's Lifeguard and Regiment of Horse and Lord Grey's Regiment, followed cautiously, from time to time firing their 'great guns' without evident effect. At around sunset, about 3 miles beyond Stow, the Royalists made another stand and, as a Parliamentarian account related:

> ...we fired at them a great while, marching up towards them five or six Regiments together, all in a body, about 800 or 1000 abrest, sixe deep, we having roome enough, it being a brave champion country; which goodly shew did so much the more daunt the enemy, that (as it is reported) Prince Rupert swore, hee thought all the Round-heads in England were there.[35]

The massed phalanx of Parliamentarian infantry was safe from attack by the Royalist horse, and at about nine in the evening skirmishing died down, with the Parliamentarian relief force now within a dozen miles of Gloucester. For once the Londoners were unconcerned about the discomforts of their bivouac:

> ...we lay all in the open field, upon the plowed land, without straw, having neither bread nor water. Yet God enabled our Souldiers to undergoe it cheerfully, there was not one feeble sicke person among us, but was able to march with us the day following.[36]

Royalist hopes of preventing the Parliamentarians from reaching Gloucester had clearly been dashed, and they saw no point in fighting another action so close to the city. Essex's methodical use of foot, horse and artillery in combination had frustrated Rupert's plans. Considerable recrimination would follow, with Rupert attempting to blame 'want of courage' by Wilmot, though others suggested that the Prince himself, and by implication Lord Forth and the King, were equally at fault for their failure, with relatively fresh troops, to engage Essex in the Vale of Gloucester before he could enter the town. However the day after the action at Stow (5 September) King Charles himself wrote to Rupert:

> Nephew,
>
> The General is of opinion that we shall do little good upon this Town, for they begin to countermine us, which will make it a work of time; whereof he is of opinion, to which I fully concur, that we should endeavour to fight with Essex as soon as may be, after we have gotten our forces together, which I hope will be tomorrow, those from Bristol being already come, the greatest care will be to meet with him before he can reach the hedges, now if this be your opinion as it is ours, which I desire to know with all speed, I desire you to do all things in order to it, that no time be lost.[37]

The troops from Bristol referred to, regiments from the force led there by Prince Rupert (whose ranks had now been partially filled out with new recruits, though still only averaging about 300 rank and file), had been the subject of a letter a few days previously from Hopton to Rupert:

> I have with all the expedition that may be sent to your Highness the five regiments of foot and one of horse, according to your orders, and I hope your Highness will receive them in time, they are a handsome body of men, the foot marched by our commissarys muster 1,600 men besides officers, and the lieutenant-colonel assures me the horse are four hundred besides officers, so they may modestly pass for two thousand foot and five hundred horse.[38]

But even if the King had replaced any losses suffered during the siege of Gloucester, there proved to be too little time to bring together his army to oppose Essex on the final stage of his march.

On the evening of 5 September Essex's army reached Prestbury, on the crest of the Cotswolds to the north-east of Cheltenham and in sight of the spires of Gloucester Cathedral in the Vale of Severn below. Essex fired off cannon to alert the garrison to his approach and pressed on down the steep hill slope through the gathering dusk to quarter in the villages below. Foster's Red Regiment of the London Brigade had been given the task of escorting the wagon train in the rear:

...but before the Wagons could come to the top of the Hill, night drawing on it began to be very darke, so that our Wagons and carriages could not get downe the hill. Many of them were overthrowne and broken, it being a very craggy steep and dangerous hill, so that the rest of the Wagons durst not adventure to goe downe, but stayed all night there: sixe or seven horses lay dead there the next morning that were killed by the overthrow of the Wagons: our Red Regiment having charge of the Wagons, were constrained to lye all night upon the top of this mountaine, it being a most terrible tempestuous night of winde and raine, as ever man lay out in, we having neither hedge nor tree for shelter, nor any sustenance of food, or fire: we had by this time marched sixe daies with very little provision for no place where we came was able to receive our Army, we leaving the Rode all the way and marching through poore little villages: our souldiers in their marching this day would run halfe a mile or a mile before, where they heard any water was...[39]

The Londoners' wretched night was made still more miserable by constant alarms of Royalist activity:

...about midnight we had two Alarmes upon this hill, in the midst of all the storme and raine, which together with the darknesse of the night made it so much the more dreadfull, which also caused a great distraction among our Souldiers, everyone standing upon his guard, and fearing his fellow Souldier to be his Enemy.[40]

One soldier was shot dead by mistake, and next morning the disconsolate Londoners finally stumbled down the hill, to find little hope of comfort:

...being wet to the very skin, but could get little or no refreshing every house being so full of Souldiers. The Cavaleers were neere the Towne with a greate body of horse: We were all presently drawne up into a body in the field; our souldiers began to complain pitifully, being worn out and quite spent for want of some refreshing, some complaining they had not eat or drinke in two dayes, some longer tyme...[41]

But if the spirits of some of Essex's weary men were drooping, the defenders of Gloucester were exultant. It is unclear when they first learnt that Essex was marching to their relief, but on 4 September they saw clear evidence of his approach when the besiegers began to load their wounded onto boats for transportation by river to Bristol. Next morning:

...we perceived their foote and horse marching after, yet we were not assured of their raysing of their siege, or that reliefe was so nere at hand, till we perceived their rere guard to fire their hutts, and their men to be drawne out of their trenches...[42]

With the Royalists in retreat, Essex saw no need to put his exhausted men to the ordeal of a trial by battle, and it would be another two days before his relief force actually entered Gloucester. The siege had been raised and the first part of Essex's march successfully completed. But he had still to get back safely to London, and few doubted what a formidable task that would be.

3

The Race for Newbury
7–19 September 1643

Making a wide circuit north-eastwards via Painswick, on 7 September King Charles established his headquarters at Sudeley Castle, about 15 miles north-east of Gloucester and firmly astride Essex's most likely return road to London.

The failure to capture Gloucester led to a storm of recriminations in the Royalist camp, which were still echoing years later when Clarendon wrote his account of events:

> The siege of Gloucester was not believed to have been well conducted, and that it might have been taken in half the time they were before it, if it had been skilfully gone about...this clamour against that engagement was so popular and universal, that no man took it upon himself to speak in defence of it... [it was] the ruin of the King's affairs.[1]

With his frequently-attested dislike of soldiers, Clarendon placed the blame squarely upon the King's senior commanders, commencing with the Lord General, Ruthven:

> The General, though he had been without doubt a very good officer, and had great experience, and was still a man of unquestionable courage and integrity; yet he was now much decayed in his parts, and with the long continued custom of immoderate drinking, dozed in his understanding, which had been never quick and vigorous, he having been always illiterate to the greatest degree that can be imagined... He was a man of few words, and of great compliance, and usually delivered that as his opinion, which he foresaw would be grateful to the King.[2]

Clarendon probably exaggerates the degree of Ruthven's incapacity. He was typical of the school of hard-drinking tough old Scottish professional soldiers who played a major role in the forces of both sides, particularly in the opening years of the war, and there is no real evidence to suggest any serious weakening of his abilities at this stage. However Ruthven may have

1 Bristol Castle. The capture of Bristol gave the Royalists a major port. But the losses incurred in the assault horrified King Charles and caused him to forbid a similar attack on Gloucester.

2 'Cavaliers and Roundheads'. This contemporary portrayal symbolising the opposing sides is nearer to the reality than many versions. In practice most supporters of King and Parliament were virtually identical in dress.

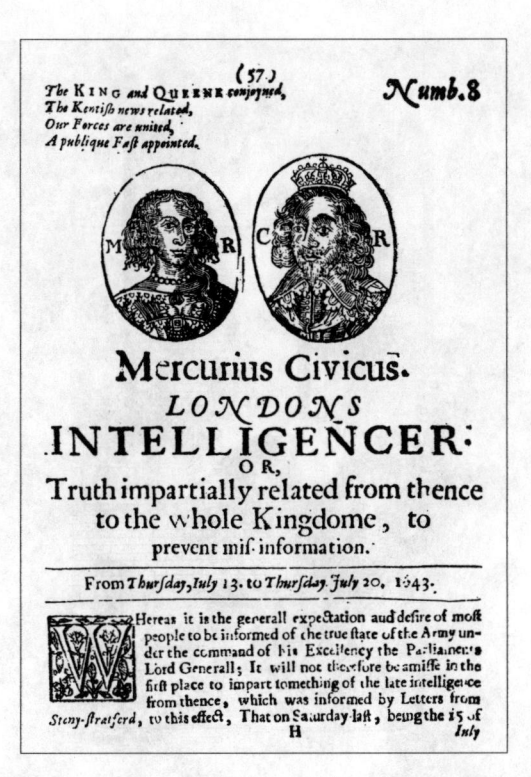

3 This Parliamentarian newsbook reports the arrival of Queen Henrietta Maria and her munitions convoy to join the King.

4 Ludlow Castle. Royalist troops were called in from a wide area to reinforce the main field army. They included Michael Woodhouse's Regiment of Foot from Ludlow.

5 Robert Devereux, Earl of Essex (1591–1646). Appointed Parliament's Captain General on the outbreak of war, Essex had not so far distinguished himself in command. The relief of Gloucester and the Newbury campaign represented his most difficult challenge so far, and probably his last chance to avoid the loss of his command.

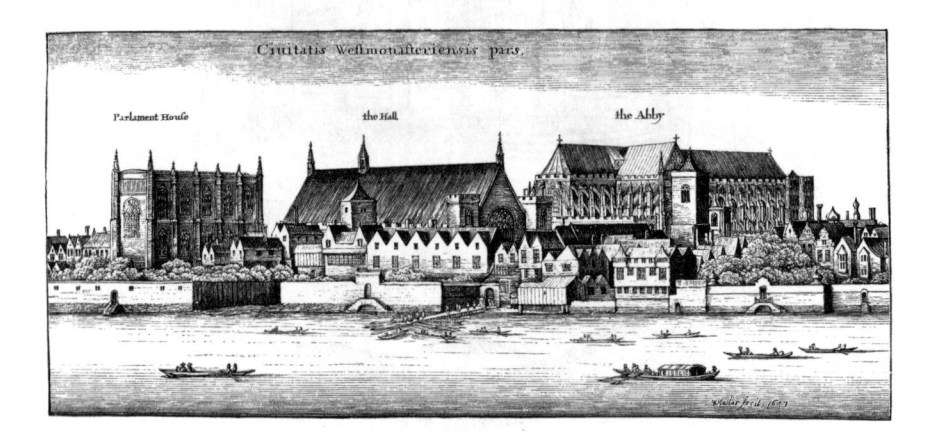

6 Westminster. St Stephen's Chapel, where Parliament met, and Westminster Hall.

7 John Pym (1584–1643). Principal leader and organiser of the Parliamentarian war effort, by the autumn of 1643 Pym was fatally ill. His final, and ultimately decisive, act was to instigate Parliament's alliance with the Scots.

8 Sir Jacob Astley (1579–1652) A highly experienced soldier, especially skilled in commanding foot, Astley had distinguished himself in the role during the Scots Wars, and became Major General of Foot of the Oxford Army in 1642.

9 At the same time as the king's forces were besieging Gloucester, the Northern Royalist army of the Earl of Newcastle was preparing to lay siege to the other key Parliamentarian garrison of Kingston upon Hull.

10 Indiscipline was an on-going problem in most Civil War armies. Whilst there were no large-scale mutinies during the Newbury campaign, desertion was a major worry, particularly for the Royalists.

11 This contemporary illustration depicts the variety of dress and equipment amongst troops. Some of the South Wales Trained Band units in the Royalist army may have been poorly equipped.

12 A musketeer, with a bandolier of powder charges and matchlock musket.

13 This contemporary cartoon of an English soldier in Ireland lampoons the widespread looting which was an inevitable feature of the behaviour of most armies.

14 This contemporary print possibly depicts dragoons firing from horseback. Normally, however, they dismounted and fought on foot.

15 Cornet of Captain Vivers of Arthur Goodwin's Regiment of Horse (Parliamentarian). Field 'tenne' (tawney orange) Motto: 'My Life and Everything to Truth' on gold or silver shield.

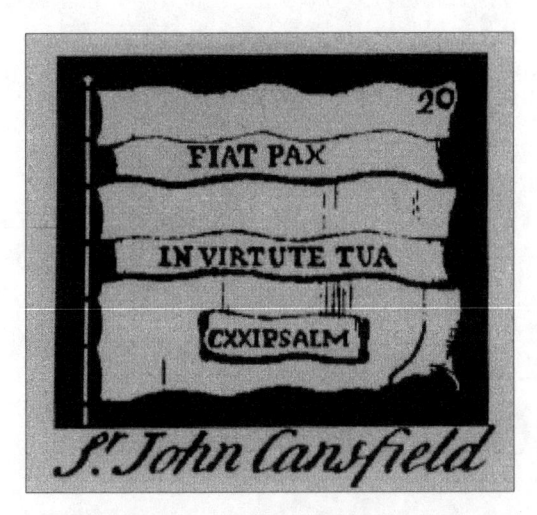

16 Cornet of Lieutenant-Colonel John Cansfield of the Queen's Regiment of Horse (Royalist). Motto: 'Peace be within thy walls'. Colour unknown.

17 Royalist cornet, possibly of an officer from Lord Spencer's Regiment of Horse, captured at Cirencester. Motto: 'I shall find or make quiet'. Field: red.

18 Cornet of Major William Boswell, (Spencer's Horse) taken at Cirencester. It depicts a Roundhead in green breeches riding away from a Royalist in a green coat and red sash. The Roundhead is calling 'Quarter'. Motto: 'He who follows conquers'. Field: red.

19 Cornet of Royalist Major Christopher Wormsley (Sir Nicholas Crispe's Regiment of Horse), killed at Cirencester. Motto: 'I hope for better things'. Woman representing 'Hope' in blue with gold wings, standing on a skeleton ('Death'). Field: white.

20 Musket. The matchlock musket was the weapon of up to two-thirds of the average regiment of foot.

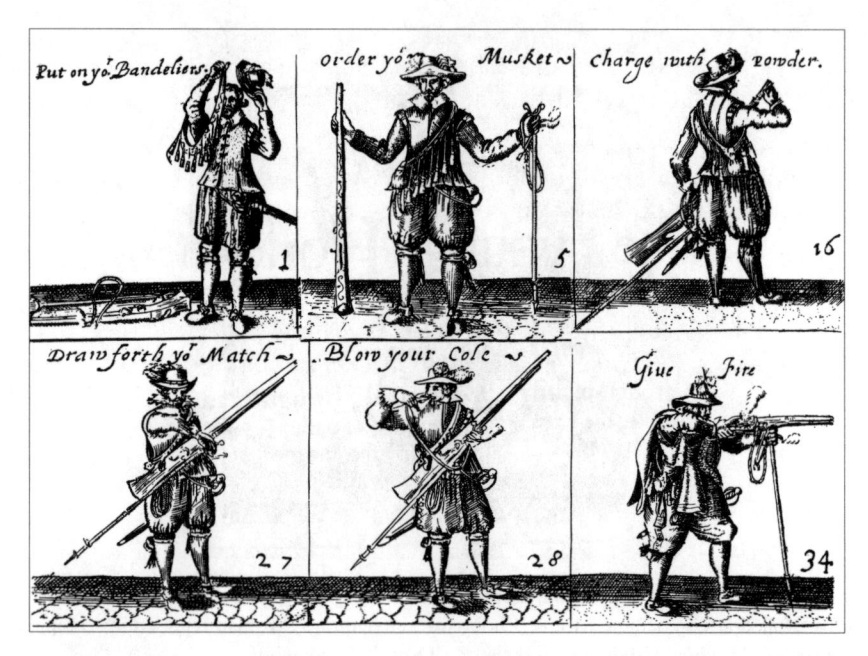

21 Musket drill as recommended in military manuals was a complex procedure. In practice it was generally considerably simplified in action.

22 Harquebusiers as depicted in John Cruso, 'Militarie Instructions for the Cavalerie', 1635, a drill book widely used during the Civil War. These troopers are fully equipped with back and breast plates, pot helmet, sword, pair of pistols and carbine.

23 Title page of a popular contemporary drill book. The fully-armoured cuirassiers depicted here were a rare sight on Civil War battlefields.

24 Pike drill was another complex procedure. In battle a major role of pikemen was to hold off attacks by enemy cavalry.

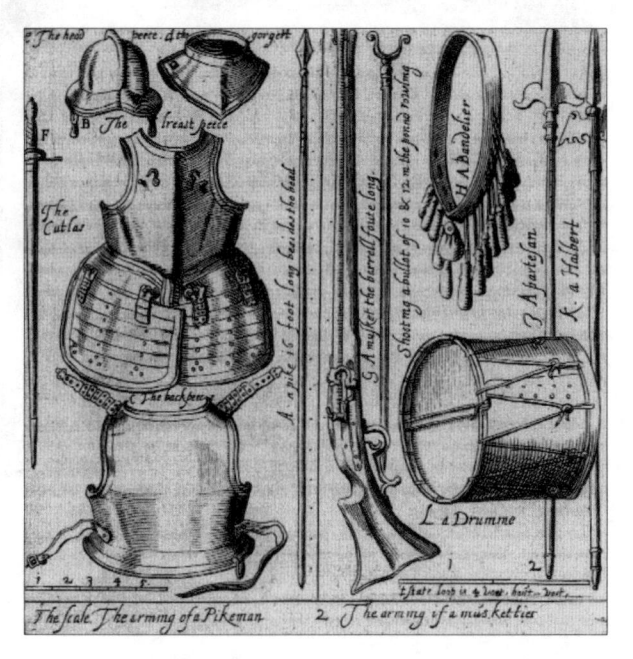

25 Infantry Equipment. On the left the recommended equipment of a pikeman. The equipment for a musketeer relates more to the earlier part of the war. As matchlock muskets became lighter and shorter, the rest was often dispensed with. The partisan on the right was often carried by officers and NCOs. These weapons and halberds were particularly useful in close-quarter fighting.

26 More contemporary images of soldiers.

27 This contemporary woodcut of the Army Council of 1647 gives a good impression of the Councils of War which were held by most Civil War armies.

28 Prince Rupert (1619–82). An outstanding cavalry commander, the King's nephew was less successful in higher command, where both his youth and foreign birth, as well as character defects hindered his effectiveness.

29 Wooden effigies of soldiers, which may be based on men of the London Trained Bands.

30 Cornet of Lord Robartes (1606–65) A supporter of Pym prior to the war, Robartes raised a regiment of foot for Essex's army in 1642, and fought at Edgehill.

31 A variety of Civil War soldiers, including an officer wearing a morion-style helmet, which was rather obsolete by 1643.

lacked the vigour needed to animate and organise an over-large Royalist army drawn together from a variety of sources and including a number of poorly trained troops with low morale.

It seems probable that the generally poor morale of the King's forces, with the most experienced of his foot still not recovered from their heavy losses in the storm of Bristol, coupled with the lack of an adequate siege train and shortages of supplies, were major factors in the failure to press the attack on Gloucester effectively. The King's commanders also discounted the ability of Essex to relieve the city. The most they expected him to do was to make an ineffective feint towards Oxford, predicting that if he attempted to advance further it would be a march in which:

> Half the King's body of horse would distress, if not destroy his whole army, and through a country eaten bare, where he could find neither provision for man nor horse; and if he should, without interruption, be suffered to go into Gloucester, he could neither stay there, nor possibly return to London, without being destroyed in the rear by the King's army.[3]

Nevertheless, the Royalist cavalry's failure to inflict the expected mauling on Essex's army during its outward march was a serious setback to the King's plans, and one for which Clarendon felt Rupert deserved a major share of the blame:

> The not engaging the Earl of Essex in all the march over so open a country, was thought inexcusable, and was imputed to the want of courage in Wilmot, whom Prince Rupert did in no degree favour, nor was the Prince himself without some reproaches, for suffering the Earl of Essex, after all the horse was joined, to march down a long steep hill into the vale of Gloucester, without any disturbance; and that the whole army, when it was found necessary to quit the siege, had not been brought to fight in that vale, and at some distance from the town, when the King's men were fresh and the other side tired with so long a march...[4]

Once again there are some grounds for Clarendon's strictures, although it seems unlikely that Rupert would have let Essex off so gently if he had really believed there had been an opportunity to inflict serious harm on him without the risk of suffering unacceptably high casualties in the process.

In any event, the Royalists had decided upon a new strategy. According to the author of the most detailed Royalist account of this phase, the King and his commanders had decided against attempting to bring Essex to battle in the enclosed country around Gloucester, where their supposed superiority in cavalry would be neutralised, but instead:

> ...rather to make choice of such a place to incamp his army as might be aptest for these three ends: to accommodate his Quarters; to strengthen him in provisions, and equally to intercept his [Essex's] flight in a faire Country, whether he should take it by way of Worcester towards Warwick or by the way of Cirencester towards Reading, and to these purposes the Towne of Winchcombe and Sudeley Castle were made chose of as the most appropriate.[5]

For his part, Essex, having entered Gloucester on 8 September to the sound of celebratory church bells, now found it necessary to halt for several days in order to allow the defenders of Gloucester time to re-provision, to rest his own exhausted men, and to consider his next move. Many of the Parliamentarian troops were quartered in the villages around Gloucester, and several skirmishes took place between them and parties of Royalist cavalry.

Foster and his London comrades were billeted for two days in the village of Norton, 3 miles from Gloucester, where at last they were able to obtain some rest and accommodation. But they were not left to enjoy it undisturbed for long; on 7 September Royalist cavalry fell on some Parliamentarian horse quartered near Winchcombe, where the regiments of Colonels Hans Behr and Arthur Goodwin were billeted. They 'killed many of them and took some Colours.' The London regiments were quartered within 2 miles, and:

> This night, about seven of the clock there came a command for our Regiments of the Trained Bands to march five miles back againe in the night but it being a very darke night, and our men worne out and spent with their marching they refused to goe.[6]

According to a Royalist account, probably referring to this same action:

> This day we had a sufficient tast how we shall deale with the Rebels Army, when ever wee can be so happy as to get it out to fight, for onely three Troopes of the Queens Regiment, commanded by the Lord Wilmot, charged 7 troops of the Rebels, and those their best Troopes too (for they were their French and Dutch, and in those they most confided) [Behr's?] and here also the Queene's Troope followed their brave Leader so like themselves, that they routed them all, killed fourscore of them in the place, tooke 30 or 40 prisoners (and which is most strange, though I can clearly say most true) lost not one man in the fight.[7]

On the same day the Royalists had another interesting success when a party of horse from Banbury captured two Parliamentarian officers, on their way from London to the Earl of Essex with a gallantry medal for one of his men:

> ...an Ovall Medall of silver gilt, hanged in an Orange tawney Ribband, on the one side of this medal is the Effigy of the Earl of Essex with a naked sword in his right hand, and over his head an Arme out of a cloud holding a sword drawne, and this circumscription: 'In the multitude of councillors is peace'.[8]

Also allegedly taken around the same time were several letters from the wives of London Train Bandsmen serving with Essex, one of which, written on 5 September by Susan Owen to her husband John Owen, marching in the Blue Regiment, encapsulated some of the fears of those who were left at home waiting for news of their loved ones:

> Most dear and tender heart, my kind affection remembered unto you; I am like never to see thee more I feare, and if you aske the reason why, the reason is this, either I am afraid the Cavaleers will kill thee, or death will deprive thee of me, being full of grief for you, which I feare will cost mee my life. I doe much grieve that you be so hard hearted to me, why could you not come home with Master Murfey on Saturday? Could you not venture as well as he? But you did it on purpose to show your hatred to me; there is none of our Neighbours with you that hath a wife but Master Fletcher and Master Norwood and yourselfe, everybody can come but you. I have sent one to Oxford to get a passé for you to come home, but when you come you must use your wits; I am afraid if you do not come home, I will much dishonour God more than you can honour him, therefore if I doe miscarry, you shall answer for it, pitty me for God's sake and come home. Will nothing prevaile with you. My cozen Jane is now with me and prays for your speedy returne, for God's sake come home, so with my prayer for you
> I rest your loving wife,
> Susan Owen[9]

Mistress Owen's fears were well grounded. As Essex and his men were only too keenly aware, although Gloucester was relieved, they were themselves in a highly precarious position. The enemy lay between them and London, and the prospect of regaining the capital without having to fight a battle on ground of the Royalists' choosing seemed very remote. The Earl had somehow to confuse the enemy about his intentions for long enough to get ahead of them in what was likely to be a race for safety. On 10 September, leaving three of his heavy guns behind in Gloucester, Essex headed north about 11 miles to Tewkesbury, the next nearest bridging point of both the rivers Severn and Avon.

News of his move reached the King at Sudeley: 'Whereby it was made probable unto us, that he intended Warwicke way.'[10] The Royalists had been awaiting supplies of ammunition which Hopton was despatching from Bristol, but it was essential to block Essex's path, so the main part of the Royalist army marched to Evesham, about 11 miles north-east of Tewkesbury, on the next crossing of the Avon, and directly on the road to Warwick.

Essex remained in the vicinity of Tewkesbury and Upton on Severn until 15 September, while opposing detachments of horse eyed each other and made probing raids. On the night of 14 September Royalist horse fell on Sir James Ramsey's Regiment of Horse which was quartered about 3 miles outside of Tewkesbury and, as Foster admitted: 'they slew many of our men and took many others prisoners. Wee took foure of them prisoners, but the greatest losse was ours.'[11]

According to *Mercurius Aulicus*:

> Prince Rupert, hearing that a considerable partie of them were quartered at a place called Oxinton, drew out a strength of Horse upon Thursday night, and went to find them in their quarters; and being come somewhat neere the place sent out one Master Fitz Williams with 30 horse to make discoverie of their posture, and returne word againe in what case he found them. The gentleman coming so neere as he might discerne them, contrary to his expectacion found them all ready armed and mounted (order being newly come from the Earle of Essex that they should presently repair unto him) and which was worse then that, a great ditch between them, so that he could not charge them in the Rere, which on his first discoverie he had meant to do. But casually looking round about him, he could discerne some other of the Rebels crosse the ditch unto their fellows, a good distance off, which made him wheele a little to obtain this passage: which having gained without resistance, he caused his men to discharge all at once upon them in the Rere, with such noyse and clamour, that the affrighted Rebels (though five Troops of Horse) betook themselves unto their heeles in a great confusion; leaving 25 of their company Prisoners, 14 dead behind them, and 50 of their Horses to be led away, in token of their strangefull cowardice. These rebellious Troops (which durst not stand to fight with 30 honest men) were Ramsay's own Regiment, Lieutenant-Generall of their Horse...[12]

Next evening, once darkness had fallen, Essex made his move. He had constructed a bridge of boats over the Severn at Upton, in the hope of persuading the Royalists that he intended to march on Worcester, but his actual initial plan was to head for Cheltenham, more or less following the course of his outward march. The Royalist *Mercurius Aulicus*, smarting at the way in which Essex had outmanoeuvred the King's forces, commented that the Earl 'stole away from his close quarters, where he had lyen so longe, in the dead of night... as one that was in great danger to be undone... with great haste, disorder and feare; no drum beating, nor trumpet sounding.'[13] The Parliamentarians had found it difficult enough to obtain supplies during their advance to Gloucester and were likely to have even more acute problems now, so when, shortly after setting out, Essex received a report of a poorly protected Royalist supply convoy quartered at Cirencester, about 16 miles to the south-east, the opportunity seemed too good to miss.

Throughout the siege Cirencester had been an important staging post for supplies, including munitions, sent from Bristol to the Royalist forces before Gloucester. The convoy currently quartered there seems mainly to have been foodstuffs and was protected as it proved inadequately, by two newly raised regiments of horse, those of Sir Nicholas Crispe and Lord Spencer. Intended to be used in an attempt to spark a new Royalist uprising in Sussex and Kent, both were under-strength and raw. Evidently they foresaw no danger that night, and had taken few precautions against attack. Some vague reports of approaching troops were taken to indicate the arrival of expected units from Prince Maurice.

Approaching Cirencester cautiously, the leading Parliamentarian troops arrived before the town in the early hours of 16 September. Somewhere between 1 and 3 a.m., they moved in to attack:

>...sending in a party of horse (under the command of Major Robert Hammond) to seize upon the Centinels and guards, while we with the rest of the horse begurt the town, and a Forlorn-hope of foot (commanded by Colonel Alex. Brackley) and his Excellencie's own Foot regiment, entered the Town, and surprised 2 Regiments of horse (being Sir Nich Crispes and Colonel Spencers) which were both by the confession of their own prisoners, intended for raising a commotion in Kent. We took there likewise 40 loads of victual, which under God's providence was the preservation of the Army till the day that we fought the great bataille; there were taken 6 standards, all the Officers except the two Colonels, which were absent, with divers other Gentlemen of quality, above 300 common Souldiers and 400 horse.[14]

Foster gives a few further details of the action:

> When we came thither Sir Robert Pye marched up to the Towne, and with some Musketteers he gave fire upon the Centinells, killed one of them and wounded the other, Sir Robert himself received a shot in the arme: the Cavaliers yielded the town and desired quarter. Wee took 225 prisoners, whereof 10 were Commanders, we tyed them two and two together with Match, and brought them along with us: we took also 27 waggon-load of provision, which the Cavaliers had provided for the reliefe of their own Army: they had taken the School-house, belonging to the Towne, and made it their store-house, to lay in such provision as they made the countrey to bring in: they slew one man of ours, who was pistolled by one that took him prisoner: we killed 2 or 3 of them.[15]

Although the townspeople of Cirencester were reputedly Parliamentarian in sympathy, the attackers took no chances on their raising the alarm. While their main force surrounded the town, the forlorn hope made its entrance, and commanded all the inhabitants upon pain of death to 'keep their dores and windowes shut, and if any man presumed to look out or crie, we were commanded to shoot them, or to knocke them done; they had let out a guard of foure men, but the Centry was asleep, whom we straight knockt down for quietnesse sake.'[16]

The Parliamentarians also took possession of about one thousand sheep and sixty cattle, previously rounded up by the Royalists, which they found in the town.

The next day, after a few hours snatched rest, a regular feature of that September for the exhausted men of both armies, the Parliamentarians marched on eastwards, the London Brigade covering about 5 miles to the village of Letton, while Essex quartered at Cricklade.

It was probably not until about daylight on the 16th that the Royalists got wind of the Parliamentarian move, the news perhaps brought by fugitives from Cirencester. The King's commanders were furious: 'they did stamp and swear and curse their Scouts exceedingly, that they gave them no better intelligence of our departure.'[17]

Essex had gained a lead of about 15 miles, effectively at least a day's march so far as the infantry were concerned, and Rupert at least saw that the main hope of intercepting, or at least delaying, the enemy march lay in prompt pursuit by the Royalist horse. Even so, it probably took several hours to bring all his cavalry together, and they were mustered on Broadway Hill, eagerly awaiting orders to pursue. But a further delay of uncertain duration occurred before the command was received from the King and Ruthven, who according to one account were eventually tracked down in a nearby cottage by an angry Rupert, who found the King quietly playing picquet with Lord Percy, watched by Ruthven! Rupert urged the need for a rapid pursuit and although Forth and Percy were reportedly unconvinced, they agreed that the Prince should be reinforced by about 1,000 hastily mounted 'commanded' musketeers from the Bristol garrison under Colonel George Lisle.

Others placed the blame for Essex's escape on Rupert. Questions were asked as to how promptly the Prince had informed King Charles of Essex's departure, while one of Rupert's brigade commanders, Sir John Byron, claimed several years later that: 'had Prince Rupert been pleased to credit my intelligence, the advantage which Essex gained might have been prevented.'[18] However by the time that he made these accusations, Byron was on bad terms with the Prince, and his claim should be viewed with caution.

While Forth and the King rounded up the infantry and guns, Rupert and his cavalry marched through the night of 16–17 September in an attempt to regain the initiative.[19]

They probably reached Cirencester early on the morning of Saturday 17 September and, as Foster learned the following day, they:

> ...had taken and killed many of our men, who stayed behind drinking and neglecting to march with their colours, who are not much to be pittied.[20]

Marching via Fairford, Lechlade and Faringdon, Rupert arrived at the village of Stanford in the Vale on the evening of the 17th.[21] The King, with the bulk of the foot, was at Alvescot, about 10 miles to the north-west, while Essex was at Swindon, about 12 miles to the south-west of Rupert, and was in increasing danger of being intercepted.

Both sides, particularly the foot, were suffering increasingly from the effects of forced marching and foul weather. The Royalist Captain John Gwynne remembered:

> And when we drew off, it proved to be a most miserable tempestuous, rainy weather, that few or none could take little or no rest on the hills where they were; and the ceasing winds next morning soon dried up our thorough-wet clothes we lay pickled in all night, (as a convenient washing of us at our coming from the trenches;) and we made such haste in pursuit of Essex's army, that there was an account given of fifteen hundred foot quite tired and spent, not possible to come up to their colours before we engaged the

enemy;... and what was worse, in most men's opinion, we were like to drop down every step we made with want of sleepe.[22]

The situation of Essex's men was of course no better. Foster recounts how on the night of 17 September the London Brigade was quartered about 2 miles to the south-east of Essex's main force, at:

> ...a little poore village called Chizleton [Chisledon], where we could get no accommodation either for meat or drink, but what we brought with us in our snapsacks; most of us quartered in the open field, it being a very cold frosty night.[23]

It is unclear what information Essex had concerning the whereabouts of the enemy. He had learnt that morning that they had reached Cirencester, but may have had no more recent news. He halted early that afternoon at Swindon, both to rest his men and to give them time to forage, and this raised Royalist hopes of intercepting the Parliamentarians who, it was now clear, would have to swing further to the south-east in order to take the London road via Newbury and Reading. On the morning of 17 September, one of the King's secretaries, John Ashburnham, had written from Northleach on the edge of the Cotswolds to Rupert:

> His Majesty hath commanded me to let your Highness know that he has altered his resolution of quartering this night at Burford, and now intends to quarter at Alvesscott at the Lady Ashcombe's house where he will be better furnished with provisions for his army, and being the straighter way will save three or four miles march. It is within 5 miles of Farringdon, whither his Majesty desires you would advertise him this night of your proceedings.[24]

That night, from Alvescot, another of the King's secretaries, Lord George Digby, sent further information to the Prince:

> ...the king hath received your Highness's letter written from [Stanford], at five o'clock this evening, and commands me, thereupon to let your Highness know, that since it appears by your intelligence that my Lord of Essex is not so far out of reach as was feared, he is desirous to make all haste towards him, his Majesty's army being all, except stragglers, well up hither to Alvescott, his Majesty's desire therefore is that if your intelligence of the Rebels not being further advanced than Cricklade continues to be true, your Highness will be pleased to send speedily your opinion which way and to what place

it will be fit for the King to march with his army tomorrow. If we looke upon the map here, supposing that Essex points for Reading, we conceive that Wantage will be the aptest place, but in this His Majesty conceives he is to be governed wholly by directions from your Highness according to your discovery of their motions, or the impressions you shall make upon them, and therefore, he desires your Highness to send him speedy advertisements of what shall conceive best... PS I am commanded to add; that you should consider to allow the foot here as much rest as can well be without losing the opportunity.[25]

On receipt of the latest information from Rupert, the Duke of Richmond replied on the King's behalf at 1 a.m. on 18 September:

I have let the King see what you have writt, who approves of all in it, and will accordingly perform his part, only desires to trace certain knowledge when Essex moved, or shall move from Cricklade, that if His Majesty's armie can arrive time enough (which he will the presently he receives the answer) he will take up his quarters at or about Wantage, so as to reach Newbury as you propose, but if that cannot be, he is loath to wearie the foot, after so great a march as they have had, which you know infers that many are left behind. Last night my Lord Digby writt to your Highness by the King's order upon the receipt of yours from Stamford to which I can add what is only known since, that besides Vavasour and some other forces, [Michael] Woodhouse will, I feel confident, come today with the Prince of Wales regiment [of foot], say 700. The motion of our armie depends much on the advertisement from you will give information...[26]

After a brief halt at Faringdon, the King and the bulk of the foot, according to his stated intention, reached Wantage on the evening of the 18th. By then Rupert had already been in action. Realising the need to slow Essex down in order for the Royalist foot to catch up and block his path at Newbury, the Prince detached a force of horse under Sir John Urrey to harry the rear of the Parliamentarian army. Meanwhile his main force of cavalry attempted to head off the enemy as they marched in a south-easterly direction, following the route of the modern A419 across the downs towards Hungerford, about 13 miles from Swindon and 8 miles from Newbury.

During the course of the morning Rupert learned from Urrey that Essex was crossing the open ground of Aldbourne Chase, and that his infantry had become badly strung out along their line of march. The bulk of the Parliamentarian horse, forming the rearguard, were nearly a mile behind them. There was therefore an opportunity to attack the isolated bodies of Parliamentarian foot before they could be supported by their horse. It was about mid-afternoon, as Essex's men crossed the downs near the village of Aldbourne just over halfway between Swindon and Hungerford, that Rupert's men caught up with them. Essex:

> ...had a sight of his Majesty's horse, which appeared in several great bodies, and were so marshalled to charge our body of foot, being then on their march in several divisions.

In the fullest Royalist version of what followed:

> ...upon the Munday morning, Colonell Urrey, with a party of a Thousand commanded men, was sent to follow them in the Reare from their quarters, while Prince Rupert with the body of the Cavalry drew over the directest way to meete him, and it was our good lucke to crosse his Army just as our party had overtaken it upon the open Downe, two miles on the north-west side of Aubourne, the Rebells decrying us drew up in Battalia, leaving only a body of some two hundred Horse upon a hill somewhat distant from the grosse of their Army, which we found meanes to steal upon with Urrie's Partie, as to charge and rout them, and taking two Coronets; and killing Forty or Fifty men, without any losse on our part; we beat them into their Foot and Cannon...[27]

The Parliamentarians admitted that:

> When the Van and body of our Army had marched almost all over Auborn Chase, there appeared about 5 or 6000 horse of the enemies, who approached hard to our Rereguard, consisting of five Regiments of Horse viz Col Middleton's, Lord Gray, Col. Sheffield, Hervey and Meldrum; their number being small, it was thought fit that they should orderly retreat to the body of the Army; but the Enemy pursuing hotly both in Rere and Flank, our retreat was not without some confusion and losse; and now being come to the body of the foot, Col. Middleton commanding the aforesaid regiments drew them up again in order, and faced the enemy, until all the foot were marched.[28]

Although the Royalists made the best of this initial success, capturing two overturned ammunition wagons as they pursued the enemy through the village of Aldbourne, they had missed their best chance of attacking Essex's foot while they were still partly unprepared and crossing a valley. Sir John Byron was unequivocal in claiming that the action had opened with:

> ...great advantage to our horse... we were so placed that we had it in our power both to charge their horse in flank and at the same time to have sent another party to engage their artillery, yet that fair occasion was omitted, and the enemy allowed to join all their forces together, and then we very courageously charged them.[29]

Certainly this failure by the Royalist horse to launch a coordinated assault gave Essex just enough time to pull his foot into closer formation and to take up position on the hillside on the far side of the valley. There seems to have been a pause of about an hour while the opposing sides eyed one another and considered their next move. According to the Royalist version of events, the Cavaliers could see:

> ...such evident symptoms of feare and distraction in their whole Army, as that the Prince was well nigh tempted from his temper, and was once resolved to have charged with three thousand horse alone; their whole Army consisting of two thousand Horse, and five thousand Foot at least, and store of Cannon. But newes arriving at the instant, that our Foot, was beyond expectation, advanced within six or seven Miles of us, it imposed upon his Highness prudence this caution, not to adventure upon half our strength, that rest, which the next day he might be sure to fight for with double power: Upon which consideration he made a stand, resolving that night onely to attend them and hinder their March.[30]

These claims are dubious in several respects. Virtually all the Parliamentarian accounts suggest that all, or nearly all, of Rupert's total force of 6–7,000 horse had actually arrived by the start of the action or soon afterwards. Once again, as at Stow-on-the-Wold during Essex's outward march, the sight of massed enemy foot in close formation had, probably correctly, been regarded by the Royalists as too formidable a proposition to attack.

During the lull which followed, parties of opposing dragoons and 'commanded' musketeers exchanged largely ineffective fire among the trees of a nearby wood and on the lower slopes of the hill. However Essex knew that if he remained in his present position, the Royalist foot were likely to join Rupert before the end of the day, and any hope of avoiding battle would be at an end. So, after firing a couple of 'drakes' or light artillery pieces at his opponents, probably at about 4 p.m. the Earl ordered his foot, guns and baggage to resume their withdrawal, giving his cavalry the vital task of holding off the enemy. The anonymous Royalist observer relates Rupert's reaction:

> We had not stood long when we discovered that the enemy prepared for a retreat and by degrees drew away their baggage first, then their foot, leaving their horse at a good distance from them.
>
> The Prince his Designe hereupon was to have charged them when halfe their Forces should have drawne off the Field into those Lanes whereinto their Baggage was already advanced, but their motions being so very slow, and the night drawing on, upon second thoughts his Highnesse judg'd it the best course to try, if (by a small party) he could ingage their horse, which was then growne to be at a good distance from their Foot. This partie he committed to the care of Urrey, with two Regiments onely neere to hand to second him, keeping the body of his horse at such a distance, as might incourage the Enemy to venture on that sever'd part, which they did with a little too much incouragement. For (to say the truth) the Regements that should have seconded Urrey, not doing theire parts so well as they ought, forced his partee to make somewhat a disorderly retreat, and the Prince to send hasty succours to them; which the Queenes Regiment (commanded by my Lord Jermyn) was ordered to doe, which his Lordship performed with much Gallantrye, being received very steadily, by a strong body of the Enemie's horse, and with a composednesse in the Officer that commanded them very remarkably. For his Lordship advancing before his Regiment, with the Marquis de la Vieuville on the one hand, and the Lord Digby on the other (the Enemies Volley of Carabines given them smartly at less than 10 yards) being past, the Commander somewhat forwarder than the rest, was plainely seen to pry into their countenances, and removing his levell [aim] from one to another to discharge his Pistoll as it were by Election at the Lord Digbye's head, but without any more hurt (saving onely the burning of his face) then hee himselfe received by my Lord Jermyn's sword, who (upon the Lord Digbye's Pistoll missing fire) ran him with it in the back, , but he was as much beholding to his Armes there as the Lord Digby to his headpiece.
>
> Immediately upon this shocke, the Queenes Regiment was so charged in the Reare by a fresh body of theirs, that the greatest part of it shifting for themselves, the Lord Jermyne, accompanied with the French Marquesse and the Officers onely of his Regiment, thought it as safe a way, as well as the most honourable, to venture forwards through their whole Army, rather than to charge back through those that had invironed him, and so with admirable successe (the unhappy losse of that gallant Marquesse excepted) he brought 4 Colours and all his Officers safe: having made their way round, through

the grosse of the enemie's foot. The Lord Digby being stonn'd, and for the present blinded with his shot, was fortunately rescued out of a Regiment of the Enemie's by a brave Charge, which Prince Rupert in person made upon them with his owne Troop, wherein his Highnesse's horse was shot in the head under him, but yet by God's blessing brought him off, and so the Enemie's horse being beaten quite to their Foot and Cannon, the night coming upon us, gave a period to the action.[31]

Once again, though possibly having slightly the worse of the actual fighting, the Parliamentarian horse had succeeded in their object of covering the withdrawal of their foot, as their account explains:

The enemy again advancing put us the second time into the like disorder, when Col. Middleton facing about towards them, with his own Regiment, two troops of my Lord of Denbigh's, and Captain Wogan's troop, charged their forlorne hope consisting of 500 horse, and put them wholly into disorder; he then charged the two Regiments that seconded the forlorn hope, and routed them; but the enemy coming on so stoutly with fresh bodies, stopt his further pursuit: then Col. Norton advancing with his own and Col. Hervey's Regiment, gave the enemy a brave charge, and was encountered with as much gallantrye on the other side, so that they both retreated at one time. Then my Lord Gray and Col. Middleton advancing on the enemy, assisted by a small party of musquetiers sent by his His Excellency out of his own Regiment commanded by Cap: Goland, put them into disorder, who not withstanding drew up again in a good strength, and made our forces retreat to the main body; at which time Sir Philip Stapleton (who had the Vanguard that day) came purposely back and drew up his Regiment to succour our forces, which caused the enemy to retreat altogether, and the night stopt any further proceedings.[32]

Thanks to the efforts of their cavalry, the Parliamentarian foot had remained unscathed. Foster later commented that only two of Essex's foot regiments actually saw any action in the encounter.

Losses are uncertain; the Parliamentarians claimed to have captured a Royalist lieutenant-colonel, two lieutenants and a cornet, themselves losing two officers killed, together with a number of common soldiers and a standard of Colonel Sheffield's. A total casualty list of about 100 for both sides may be reasonably close to the mark.

The casualty who aroused the greatest interest on both sides was the French Marquis de Vieuville, riding, like a number of his countrymen, as a volunteer with the Queen's Regiment of Horse. According to the Parliamentarians, he was captured, but:

> ...it seems he would not be known who he was, but endeavouring to rescue himself from a Lieutenant that took him Prisoner, and thereupon, having his head almost cloven asunder with a pole-axe, he acknowledged himself, in the last words he spoke, which were; 'Vous voyez un grand Marquis mourant'.[33]

According to Sergeant Foster, however, who later saw the body, Vieuville died as a result of three shots, one in the chest, one in the shoulder and the third in the face.[34]

The Parliamentarians took Vieuville's body with them that night to Hungerford, earning much disapproval from the Royalists when they demanded 300 gold pieces for its release.

The Parliamentarians pushed on into the night, suffering considerably:

> ...we were much distressed, for want of sleep as also for other sustenance. It was a night of much rain and we were wet to the skin.[35]

At about 6 a.m. on 19 September Essex's weary troops entered Hungerford. Fear of Rupert's cavalry was both slowing their march and preventing them from foraging. Rupert himself spent the night conferring with the King at Wantage, while his cavalry lay to the south of that town.

Resuming his march, Essex, probably because of fear of a renewed attack, took the road on the south side of the River Kennet, through Kintbury and Hamstead to Enbourne. He had been pushed off the main road to Newbury, and as a result lost his last chance of reaching the town before the Royalists. Some time late in the afternoon of 19 September, the vanguard of Rupert's cavalry entered Newbury, driving out some Parliamentarian quartermasters who had just reached the town. As the Royalist foot steadily marched down from Wantage to support the horse, the King and his commanders knew that they had achieved their first objective. They had firmly blocked the road to London, and Essex would have no option but to fight.

4

The Armies

Until fairly recent times, the impression often given of the armies of the English Civil War was one of semi-trained amateur soldiers, officered by men little more skilled or experienced than those they commanded, from which Parliament's war-winning professional New Model Army gradually emerged. This is in fact a significant distortion of the actual position in 1642.

So far as the rank and file of the armies raised by King and Parliament is concerned, before the war all the male population between the ages of sixteen and sixty had been liable for service in the county militias and Trained Bands. The latter were intended to be composed of men of somewhat higher social standing, usually those who owned or rented land, and were therefore regarded as having a vested interest in preserving social order or repelling foreign invaders. Although the standard of equipment and training of these units varied widely from one area to the next, depending largely on the degree of apparent threat and the availability of wealthy patrons, the best of the Trained Bands, such as those of London, were of a relatively high quality, their effectiveness limited mostly by a frequent unwillingness to serve far from home.

The London Trained Bands, who played a major role in the Newbury campaign, owed much of their effectiveness to the enthusiasm of some of the city's leading merchants, who, before the war, formed a voluntary association known as the Society of the Artillery Garden. Its members took a keen interest in continental military theory and practice, and employed professional soldiers to train them. Before the war their principal training officer was Philip Skippon, who early in 1643 was made Sergeant-Major General in Essex's army.

In February 1642 the London Trained Bands had been organised into six regiments, totalling 8,000 men. In 1643 the suburbs of the City of Westminster, Southwark and Tower Hamlets were added, each with its own Trained Band regiment. To these were added nine auxiliary regiments, giving a total of eighteen in all. Two regiments of horse were also raised, making in all about 20,000 foot and 1,000 horse. The units which marched with Essex were selected by drawing lots.

The men of the Trained Bands provided their own arms and equipment, though they evidently wore civilian clothes. In an attempt at uniformity some seem to have acquired sleeveless buff coats.

Some of these existing units, such as several of the Yorkshire Trained Band regiments conscripted by the King, formed the cadres of regiments in the armies raised in 1642. The majority of conscripts, or 'volunteers', a distinction which was often in practice considerably blurred, had at least some basic military training.

There was also considerably more experienced officer material available than sometimes realised. Thousands of Scots had served in the Thirty Years' War, usually, though by no means always, on the Protestant side, and the Scottish professional soldier found ready employment with both King and Parliament on the outbreak of the Civil War. Men such as Patrick Ruthven for the Royalists, John Middleton with the Earl of Essex and John Urrey at different times for both, brought a wealth of experience and expertise to bear in training, advising and commanding the newly raised armies.

Nor were these, and some European 'mercenary' experts whose services were eagerly sought, unique. It had for many years been common for younger men from the nobility and gentry classes to spend a few years serving as volunteers in the continental wars, predominantly fighting for the Dutch in the Low Countries. There were many such men in the armies which met at Newbury, including Essex himself. At Edgehill in 1642 over sixty Parliamentarian officers could be classed as professional soldiers, together with at least thirty of those who fought for King Charles.

The rapid expansion of the armies which followed the failure of the 1642 campaign to bring the war to its expected speedy conclusion meant that many officers in newly raised units started off as 'amateurs' in the true sense of the word. But the realities of active service meant that, if they survived, they did not remain such military innocents for long. Furthermore, there were a number of widely available, relatively elementary, drill books, which fairly quickly enabled any new officer of average ability to instil the elements of military knowledge and discipline both into himself and, to a greater or lesser extent, into the men under his command.

By the time of the Newbury campaign, while not yet approaching the 'professionalism' of some contemporary continental forces, or the level of experience reached in the final years of the Civil War, the opposing armies contained ample numbers of men of all ranks who were at least competent practitioners of the art of war.

Cavalry – 'the horse' – were still seen as the 'queen' of the battlefield, the elite arm which would decide the outcome of a contest. Most contemporary military writers recommended that an army should have a horse/foot ratio of 1:2. Even at the start of the war this aim was rarely realised, and in practice a number of factors, including the generally higher rate of desertion among the foot, meant that the proportions were often reversed. In the later stages of the Newbury campaign, after his infantry had suffered severely from the results of attrition, the King probably had roughly equal numbers of horse and foot, though Essex, whose army had been reinforced and reorganised just before the Gloucester march, more nearly approached the recommended proportions.

Military writers recognised three main types of cavalry. Most highly regarded was the cuirassier, a heavy horseman wearing three-quarter-length armour and mounted on a heavy charger. These chargers were costly and difficult to obtain and maintain, while the armour was also expensive and uncomfortable, and not very effective in withstanding musket shot (though more resistant to pistol fire). The only full-strength unit to have been maintained for long as cuirassiers were Sir Arthur Haselrigge's Regiment of 'Lobsters' which served with Sir William Waller during the summer campaign in the west. But by late 1643, with the possible exception of a handful of small units such as Essex's Lifeguard, three-quarter armour was generally restricted to a few senior officers.

Lancers were widely used on the Continent, but in England a few abortive attempts to raise units of them seem to have come to nothing, and they were only employed by the Scots.

The standard cavalryman of the English Civil War was the third type – the 'harquebusier'. Technically classed as light cavalry, the troopers on both sides were by late 1643 equipped and armed in similar fashion. They were protected by back and breast plates of iron, and one out of a number of variations of the 'pot' helmet. Some at least were provided with buff coats of varying quality, made from hardened leather or hide. Cavalry were armed with a sword and a pair of pistols and frequently with a short musket or carbine.

In the earlier stages of the war there had been a marked difference in the tactics employed by Parliamentarian horse and their counterparts in the main Royalist field armies. Partly perhaps because of an initial shortage of firearms, in 1642 Rupert and his cavalry commanders adopted cuirassier tactics for his harquebusiers. They were employed in the role of heavy cavalry, formed three ranks deep, and used shock tactics modelled on those used with considerable effect by the Swedes during the Thirty Years' War. Approaching the enemy at a 'good round trot', rather than the headlong charge of popular legend, the Royalist troopers would discharge one of their pistols at close range before engaging the enemy in hand-to-hand combat.

For approximately the first twelve months of the war, the Parliamentarian horse continued to place reliance upon the more traditional 'Dutch' tactics. These relied upon firepower, from units formed four ranks deep, to break the impact of an enemy attack, and by implication meant that troops using them tended to stand on the defensive. On the whole these tactics proved less successful than those of the Royalists. Certainly the Royalist cavalry began the war with a clear qualitative 'edge' over their opponents, though the tactics employed by their opponents were not necessarily as ineffective as the early showing of the Parliamentarian horse might suggest. They did however require well-trained and steady troops who would stand their ground in the face of an enemy attack, and this, all too often, the Parliamentarian horse in the early months of the war proved unable to do.

However as their experience, training and confidence improved the Parliamentarian cavalry, still at first predominantly using the same tactics with which they had begun the war, proved increasingly tough opponents. As early as the action at Chalgrove Field (18 June 1643) the Royalists were noting that the enemy horse were standing their ground more effectively, and the trend continued throughout the summer. Increasingly, Parliamentarian cavalry commanders were also beginning to adopt similar tactics to the Royalists, though it seems unlikely that these innovations had progressed far in Essex's army by the time of Newbury. They were still outclassed, but were much tougher opponents than had been the case at Edgehill a year earlier.

The basic tactical unit of the cavalry was the troop, numbering an average of about sixty troopers, four officers (captain, lieutenant, quartermaster and cornet) and two trumpeters, with NCOs and a farrier. Although they might operate independently it was more usual for a number of troops, theoretically about six to ten, to be formed together into regiments, with a recommended strength of about 500 troopers plus officers. In practice establishments varied widely, with popular commanders such as Prince Rupert having no difficulty in maintaining regiments much larger than the average, while other less wealthy or successful commanders often failed to keep their regiment in existence.

Although the difference is often exaggerated, Royalist cavalry regiments probably included a slightly higher number of men of gentry origin than did those of their opponents. But the majority of troopers on both sides were from a wide range of more humble origins. As well as the expected farmers, husbandmen, grooms and other outdoor servants, many townsmen might also be found in the ranks, which was not unexpected in age when the majority of the male population had at least some basic skill in horsemanship.

A foot regiment had a theoretical establishment of 1,200 men, again organised into a basic tactical unit, the company. The company could be of varying size, and up to about ten of them would form a regiment. Military writers recommended a 1:2 pike/musket ratio, but this varied in practice. As the war went on, the proportion of musketeers tended to increase, though at Newbury the majority of units on both sides more or less followed the recommended pattern. It was common to detach parties of musketeers to form 'commanded' bodies for particular tasks, such as operating with cavalry or acting as skirmishers. One such unit in the Newbury campaign were the 1,000 musketeers under Lieutenant-Colonel George Lisle, apparently formed out of detachments from regiments in the Bristol garrison, which operated firstly as mounted musketeers with Rupert's horse and then as an independent foot formation at Newbury.

The pike, tracing its lineage back to antiquity, was popularly regarded as the most 'honourable' weapon. It might in theory be up to 16 foot in length, though it was more commonly cut down by about a quarter for ease of use. Pikemen had originally worn body armour, and although records exist of its issue to Essex's troops, it is unlikely that troops in either army were still wearing more than a 'morion' or 'pot'- type helmet by the time of Newbury. Pikemen relied partly on the psychological effect of the sight of their advance in a dense body, which might unnerve a poorly motivated opponent and cause him to break before contact. If this did not happen, the next phase of an encounter between opposing bodies of pikemen would involve a tactic known as 'push of pike'. This, (resembling in some ways a modern rugby 'scrum') was designed to disorganise the enemy, knock opponents off their feet and push them back in increasing disorder until they eventually broke, after which significant casualties might be inflicted. In practice, particularly if both sides were poorly motivated or unenthusiastic, such contests often degenerated into deadlocked 'fencing matches', with soldiers ineffectually flourishing or clashing their pikes.

The other major role of pikemen was to provide a defence against cavalry attack. Musketeers might if possible shelter under the protection of a 'hedgehog' formed by the pikemen, who, with their pikes 'charged' to receive horse, could partially hold off the attackers while the musketeers defended themselves with their shot or clubbed musket. Once again the success of such defence would depend upon the determination with which the attack was pressed home and upon the morale and discipline of the defenders. If an infantry formation broke in such circumstances, the ensuing slaughter might be horrific.

The musketeer's standard weapon was the matchlock musket. This weapon was cheap to produce and relatively easy to use, though its firing procedure (by means of a length of burning cord known as match, used to ignite the charge) was frequently unreliable, particularly in damp conditions. The matchlock had a theoretical range of about 400 yards, although it was only really effective at a quarter of that distance or less. Contemporary drill books contain complicated loading and firing procedures, which often lead to their actual rate of fire being seriously underestimated. In practice, in combat situations a greatly simplified procedure was employed, meaning that an averagely competent musketeer could discharge his weapon approximately every thirty seconds.

Most infantry encounters, if pressed home with sufficient determination, and assuming that the opposing side did not flee or retreat, eventually became hand-to-hand engagements. In these the musketeer generally found the butt of his matchlock to be a more effective weapon than the cheap sword with which he was also normally supplied.

Musketeers were normally deployed in six ranks, each firing in succession then wheeling to the rear in order to reload. By these means a well-trained unit might be expected to keep up a virtually continuous rate of fire. Exchanges of fire in these circumstances could be quite prolonged, particularly if troops were reluctant to close with their opponents, but as with 'push of pike' it was not generally very bloody in its effects. Terrain also played a significant part in the nature of infantry combat. If, as at Newbury, the ground over which the battle was fought was heavily enclosed by thick hedgerows or areas of woodland, the ordered formations recommended by the textbooks were frequently impracticable. Instead the role of the pikeman was reduced, except against cavalry attack in the open, and the contest was fought out between smaller parties of musketeers, firing at each other from cover and not suffering particularly heavy casualties unless they met in hand-to-hand fighting. Such situations also made it difficult for officers to force poorly motivated or exhausted men into serious action.

Although foot in regional armies often went to war wearing their own civilian clothing, attempts were made to clothe the infantry of the main field armies in a more uniform fashion. In August, Essex's men were issued with red or grey coats, while in the previous month the Royalist foot regiments in Oxford were provided with either red or blue suits and montero caps.

Also present at Newbury in the ranks of both armies were dragoons. These were best described as mounted infantry, who rode to the scene of action and then fought dismounted. Armed with short-barrelled musket and sword, they were chiefly employed on such occasions in a skirmishing role to clear enemy outposts and to provide fire support for cavalry.

Artillery received much attention from military writers, and had already played a significant role in some contemporary engagements in Europe. In the Civil War, however, its main significance was generally to be found in siege operations. This was partly because of limited numbers of suitable guns and inadequate expertise in using them, and also because of the enclosed nature of the terrain over which many battles were fought. There were occasions, however, when cannon did play a noteworthy part in battle, and Newbury was to be one of them. The heaviest guns, whole cannon of about sixty-three pounds and the slighter lighter demi-cannon and culverin, were more generally reserved for siege work because of their slow rate of fire, although the King seems to have emplaced at least one such battery at Newbury. More use was made of the lighter guns, the medium-rated demi-culverin, and the lighter pieces, averaging a shot weight of three pounds or less, which went under a variety of names such as drakes, sakers and falcons, and which were primarily anti-personnel weapons.

The artillery formed part of the Train, an organisation which came under the General of the Ordnance, and was fairly wide-ranging in its scope, including in its personnel not only a small number of trained gunners and their assistants, the latter known as 'matrosses', but also explosive experts termed 'fireworkers' and the various drivers and 'conductors' responsible for the vast train of wagons. Also coming under the control of the General of the Ordnance were the pioneers, miners and the various craftsmen, blacksmiths and the like. There were a wide variety of ancillary personnel, for the Train was not merely responsible for ordnance, but also controlled supplies of munitions of all kinds, as well as such necessities as tools and horseshoes.

By the time they met at Newbury, both armies were at the end of a long and arduous campaigning season which had taken a severe toll on them. Although the armies were broadly similar in organisation and equipment, it is worth looking in a little more detail at the forces of King and Parliament as they prepared to meet in battle at Newbury.

At the start of the siege of Gloucester, King Charles may have been at the head of the biggest Royalist army ever mustered during the war. Although estimates of a total strength of 30,000 may be too high, he almost certainly had at least two thirds of that total available. But by the time that Essex was brought to bay outside Newbury, the Royalist army was considerably smaller. An unknown number of casualties had been incurred during the operations at Gloucester, while desertion and losses through sickness were also significant. Once the siege was raised the King evidently returned at least some of the troops from the Midlands to the garrisons from which they had been drawn, although these were partially compensated for by other reinforcements including the strong Prince of Wales Regiment of Foot under Michael Woodhouse. The King's forces were further depleted by straggling during the pursuit of Essex, with estimates that at least 1,500 were still adrift when the battle began. Clarendon reckoned that Rupert commenced the campaign with about 8,000 horse,[1] which seems likely to be a reasonably accurate figure. Allowing for depletion of various kinds, there were probably still about 7,000 available at Newbury. The foot, particularly the regiments of the Oxford Army, had however dwindled considerably in the course of their summer campaign, with losses incurred at Bristol not fully replaced, and other subtractions since. Charles may have begun the fight with approximately 8,000 infantry.

The Royalist artillery train consisted of two demi-cannon, two culverins, two twelve-pounder demi-culverins, five six-pounders, one saker, two minions, four three-pounders and two 'base'. Significantly, he had considerably fewer light anti-personnel type guns than did his opponents.

At first glance the Royalists might appear to have enjoyed the advantages of a clear command structure. King Charles I, Captain-General and theoretically undisputed head of the Royalist forces, was, after all, present in person. The reality, however, was much less satisfactory. As with virtually all armies of the period, major strategic and operational decisions were taken at a Council of War, and it was in these situations that fundamental weaknesses in the Royalist direction of the war became apparent. The Council of War was made up of the King and senior civilian and military figures. As with most similar bodies, it had no executive powers but was intended to act in an advisory capacity, final decisions resting with the King. Its membership varied, but normally the Council included high-ranking officers; the Lord General (Patrick Ruthven), the General of Horse (Prince Rupert), the Lieutenant-General of Horse (Lord Wilmot), the Major-General of Foot (Sir Jacob Astley) and, when present, the General of the Ordnance (Lord Percy). Also attending, in smaller numbers on campaign than when in Oxford, were civilian officials such as the Secretary of State (Lord Falkland) and the Chancellor of the Exchequer (Edward Hyde). Various currently favoured courtiers with no clear official position, such as the King's cousin, the Duke of Richmond, might also be present, along with various 'experts', normally lower-ranking military officers. On average the Council numbered between ten and seventeen, generally fewer when on campaign, when it might be expected to meet daily.

A number of factors worked against the smooth and effective running of the Royalist Council of War. First and most damaging was the character of King Charles himself. A fatal mixture of stubbornness and irresolution, the King wavered between conflicting sources of advice, tending to favour advice offered by those currently in favour, regardless of its value. With no previous military experience, he was also notoriously incapable of controlling or mediating between the opposing factions in the Royalist high command and court, whose differences frequently came to a head in Council.

Not only were there ongoing disputes and distrust between civilians and soldiers, but each of these groupings were in turn riven by dissension. Most significant for the course of events in the Newbury campaign were the differences affecting the military commanders.

Opinions differed regarding the effectiveness of Patrick Ruthven, the Lord General (effectively the King's military adviser and chief of staff responsible for the day-to-day operations of the army). Aged about seventy, Ruthven was a vastly experienced professional soldier who had been highly regarded by so able a judge as King Gustavus Adolphus of Sweden, and almost certainly deserves more credit for the successes of the Oxford Army than he is often given. However he was apparently suffering increasingly from the effects of age, old wounds, a more recent slight wound suffered at Gloucester, and ill-health (especially gout). It was these, rather than his renowned fondness for the bottle, which by 1643 were perhaps slowing Ruthven's reactions when dealing with a fast-moving situation like the operations leading up to the Battle of Newbury.

Prince Rupert, at the age of twenty-four, was the most prominent figure in the Royalist Army. He had limited pre-war military experience, cut short by capture by the Imperialists at the Battle of Lemgo (1638) and subsequent incarceration in Austria. As a result, although in 1642 Rupert was widely read on the art of war, knowledge mostly acquired during his imprisonment, his practical experience of command was limited, and he was held by many to owe his appointment as General of Horse more to being the King's nephew than to any proven military ability.

In the event Rupert had proved to be an outstandingly able and charismatic leader. Though his exact part in devising the tactics which were adopted with such success by the Royalist horse remains unclear, Rupert's leadership played a major part in their string of successes in the opening months of the war. But Rupert's undisputed ability on the field of battle was counterbalanced by other factors, frequently injurious both to his uncle's cause and to himself. His relative youth and inexperience did not prevent Rupert from having strong and forcefully expressed opinions, while his natural intolerance for the views of others, and his semi-foreign birth, helped alienate many of those with whom he had dealings.

Generally Rupert seems to have been on reasonably amicable terms with Ruthven, who either acquiesced with or found means to circumvent the Prince's opinions. But it seems that the two disagreed on a number of occasions during the Newbury campaign, firstly over the conduct of operations at Gloucester and later over what Rupert saw as Ruthven's tardiness in pursuing Essex.

Rupert was also on increasingly bad terms with his Lieutenant-General of Horse, Henry, Lord Wilmot. Wilmot was a capable professional soldier in his own right, with considerably more pre-war military experience than Rupert, and he had commanded the Oxford Army horse with a fair degree of success when Rupert was absent, notably at the sweeping victory in July at Roundway Down. It seems that Wilmot increasingly resented what he saw as interference from the Prince, and when Rupert, never slow to scapegoat others for possible weaknesses on his own part, blamed Wilmot for the failure to prevent Essex from relieving Gloucester, relations deteriorated further.

Major-General of Foot in the Oxford Army was Sir Jacob Astley, another vastly experienced professional soldier who had served for many years in the Low Countries and had been Prince Rupert's military tutor before assuming the leadership of the King's infantry first in the Scots Wars and then on the outbreak of the Civil War: 'a command he was very equal to, and had exercised before, and executed with great approbation'.[2] Astley was highly competent at his job: 'Honest, brave, plain, prompt in giving orders, cheerful in any action, and as fit for the office he exercised as Christendom yielded.' He was not however noted for his contributions at the Council of War, where he 'rather collected the ends of debates, and what he was himself to do, rather than enlarged them by his own discourse, though he forbore not to deliver his own mind'.[3]

Henry, Lord Percy, General of the Ordnance, has often been criticised for his performance in general and especially in the Newbury campaign. Much of the real work of his department was carried out by his capable deputy, Sir John Heydon, and it may be that Percy's actual influence, whether for good or ill, was in practice fairly limited.

It is unlikely that the King's civilian advisers had much input into the operational decisions reached during the Newbury campaign. The principal Secretary of State, Lucius Cary, Earl of Falkland, was a man of sensitivity and intelligence and a lover of peace, who had found himself increasingly in despair as the war spread and intensified. By the time of Newbury his mood was one of deep depression.

The size of the Parliamentarian army at Newbury is also uncertain. Essex's army had been severely understrength in the early summer, but it had been reinforced both by new levies and by the contingent from the London Trained Bands. Some depletion from various causes had occurred in the course of the campaign, and it is probably safe to assume that at Newbury it was roughly equal to, or possibly slightly smaller, than the Royalist army.

Essex had about 4,000 horse, giving the King a clear advantage in this arm, and perhaps 9,000 foot. The strength of his artillery train is unknown but it must have at least equalled that of the King, and included a strong contingent with the London Brigade.

Robert Devereux, 2nd Earl of Essex, had been Parliament's Captain-General and commander of its principal field army since the start of the war. His pre-war military experience had been limited to brief service in the Palatine, the inglorious Cadiz expedition of 1625 and the equally unsuccessful Scots War of 1639, in which he was second-in-command. His performance had remained no more than adequate in the opening campaigns of the Civil War, with failure to defeat the King at Edgehill or to bar his path to London, followed by passive success in the stand-off at Turnham Green, which turned back the Royalist advance. Essex had received his training in the Dutch school of military theory, whose cautious and methodical approach matched his own personality.

Essex's main success in the earlier operations of 1643 had been his capture of Reading in May. But further moves aimed at taking Oxford had foundered in the Thames Valley, amidst disease which decimated his ranks and much mutual recrimination between Essex, his fellow commanders and the Parliamentarian leadership.

In character Essex was personally brave, but quick to take offence and lacking in both strategic insight and the ability to take rapid decisions. With some justification, by the summer of 1643 Essex saw his position as being under threat both from rivals such as Sir William Waller and from the more radical pro-war faction in Parliament. On the eve of the Battle of Newbury, for the second time in his career forced to fight with the enemy between him and home, Essex faced a situation which would make or break both himself and his army.

Lieutenant-General of Horse was Sir Philip Stapleton. Noted as being 'of a thin body and weak constitution, but full of spirit', Stapleton had little if any pre-war military experience. As an influential member of the House of Commons, titular commander of Essex's Lifeguard of Horse and colonel of a regiment of horse, he might be seen as a political appointment. Perhaps equally influential with regard to the cavalry of Essex's army was Colonel John Middleton, another of the ubiquitous Scottish professional soldiers who played such an important role in the armies of the period. Originally a colonel of dragoons, he had been transferred to the horse after their poor showing at Edgehill, and had performed creditably throughout the earlier stages of the Newbury campaign.

Probably the most able, and arguably the most influential, of Essex's senior commanders was his Major-General of Foot, Philip Skippon. Of fairly humble origins, Skippon had begun his military career as a pikeman with the English forces in the Palatinate, later gaining a notable reputation as a military instructor and as commander of the London Trained Bands in the opening months of the war, before being appointed that winter as Essex's Major-General of Foot. A tough professional soldier, Skippon had the warm regard of his men, in whose welfare he took a keen interest, being the author of a book of religious devotions for the troops, 'with rude verses interspersed' to keep their attention!

The evidence suggests that Skippon took the leading role in advising Essex at Newbury, and in directing many of the actions of his army.

5
Newbury
Approach to Battle

As the opposing armies gathered around the town on the evening of 19 September 1643, Newbury's few thousand inhabitants must have counted themselves particularly unfortunate to have been caught up in the front line of the Civil War.

Newbury was primarily a woollen-manufacturing and market town, whose townsfolk, though probably predominantly Parliamentarian in sympathy, had hitherto played little part in the war. The bulk of the town was situated on the southern bank of the River Kennet, crossed by a bridge, and consisted principally of two main streets extending southwards for about a mile. The strategic importance of Newbury lay in its bridge over the Kennet and in the fact that it dominated two major roads to London from the west via Reading. The more important route on the north bank of the Kennet was also controlled by Donnington Castle, which lay a mile to the north.

On 19 September Essex and his army had been forced to march along the southern route, on the south bank of the river, and this meant that the now inevitable battle would be fought to the west of Newbury in the area extending some 4 miles southwards from the Kennet to the River Enbourne.

On the southern bank of the Kennet, traversed by the Enbourne Road, were flat flood plains, extending southwards for about a mile until they reached a ridge of higher ground, running roughly from east to west. At the western end of this area, which went under the name of Guyer's Field, were a number of small, hedged enclosures associated with the village of Enbourne.

The higher ground to the south was the most striking feature of the immediate area. Of key importance in the battle, though neither side apparently immediately appreciated the fact, would be a blunt-nosed spur extending in a north-easterly direction towards Newbury, known to history as 'Round Hill'. Reaching a height of about 24 metres, Round Hill dominated the flood plains and the Enbourne Road.

To the south lay an area of rolling country, crossed by small lanes and tracks. Here were a number of small, thickly-hedged fields with high-banked lanes between them, particularly to the north-east, on Round Hill and towards Newbury. Another ridge of higher ground ran southwards towards the River Enbourne, crossed by the southern road to Theale and Reading.

Immediately to the south of the road was an area of relatively open ground called as Wash Common, known at its western end as Enbourne Heath. It would be here that the Royalists would have the best chance of making use of their supposed superiority in cavalry.

Overall, the ground over which the battle would be fought would be best suited to a defending force, provided that it could gain possession of the higher ground. An attacker would face serious difficulties, particularly in penetrating the numerous small enclosures. It would also largely prevent the use of the usual infantry formations, recommended by the military textbooks for employment in more open terrain, and would render pikemen particularly ineffective, except in defence against cavalry. The horse would also be severely restricted in their operations.

Unfortunately for the Earl of Essex, who late on 19 September seemed in the best situation to occupy this ground, merely standing on the defensive was not likely to prevent the eventual destruction of his army.

As dusk fell that evening, Essex's men quartered for the night in the village of Enbourne and the surrounding area, about 3 miles west of Newbury. According to tradition, Essex himself spent the night in a small house known as Bigg's Cottage, roughly in the centre of what would be the Parliamentarian position next day. Although a Parliamentarian writer claimed that the troops were 'full of courage and in no way disheartened by their hard service', their mood may in fact have been nearer to one of desperation, heightened by the fact that a large quantity of much-needed supplies which had been awaiting them in Newbury were now in enemy hands.

To a neutral observer that night, all the advantages would seem to have lain with the King. He was squarely across Essex's line of march, and for the moment had a reasonably secure line of communications with his headquarters at Oxford, about 30 miles away. It might seem that all he needed to do was occupy the various key positions outside Newbury and wait for the Parliamentarian army either to be starved into submission or destroyed by fruitless frontal assaults.

In reality, the situation seems to have been much less clear-cut for the Royalist high command. Sir John Byron wrote of the day's events: 'both armies march't as if it had been for a wager, which should come to Newbury first, and it was our fortune to prevent them of that quarter, and likewise of Donnington Castle.'[1] It was then that the problems began.

It was probably late afternoon when the vanguard of Rupert's cavalry occupied Newbury and, on a day of heavy rain and gathering gloom, it may be that visibility was poor. Whether because of a lack of clear orders, fatigue, or simply confusion, there certainly seems to have been a failure to appreciate the significance of the terrain to the west of Newbury, particularly of the high ground in the vicinity of Round Hill. Byron, who may or may not have been present at the critical time, commented later:

> Here another error was committed, and that a most gross and absurd one, in not viewing the ground, though we had day enough to have done it, and not possessing ourselves of those hills above the town by which the enemy was necessarily to march the next day to Reading.'[2]

The Royalists did however send parties of horse patrolling southwards in the direction of Wash Common. An anonymous Royalist officer later wrote:

> ...the King's army being drawne upon a Heath neere Newbury, the enemy were discovered approaching the town, Prince Rupert was pleased to command mee to advance with the partye to the hill [Wash Common] upon our left hand, from thence we sent out parties all night, which gave His Highness satisfactory intelligence...[3]

A number of minor and indecisive skirmishes took place during the night between parties of opposing horse, but the Royalists evidently remained ignorant of the significance of Round Hill, at this stage still unoccupied by the enemy.

At some stage in the evening the King called a Council of War in Newbury. Accounts of the discussion are scanty, but it seems that Rupert favoured standing on the defensive and allowing the enemy to come to them. The most detailed Royalist account suggests that the King and his commanders had no clear idea what plan to adopt and deferred a decision until daylight clarified the situation:

> The Rebels thus happily overtaken in their flight consultation was held of the way to prevent their further evading us, and it was resolved on for the best to draw out all the King's Army that night into a large field on the other side of Newbury adjoining to those closes where the Enemy had made this hand; to the end we might be in readiness to presse upon the first motion of theirs. The night was past in much uncertainty, but with opinion on our part that they were marcht away...[4]

Clarendon indeed goes so far as to suggest that 'it was resolved over night not to engage in battle but upon such grounds as should give an assurance of victory.'[5]

The dawn of 20 September was to reveal some disquieting realities. Essex and his commanders were on the move early. After issuing a rather dampening proclamation to his men to the effect that they would have to fight that day against an opponent who held most of the advantages, 'the Hill, the Town, Hedges, Lane and River',[6] Essex and his commanders set to work to deploy their army.

The approximately 9,000 Parliamentarian foot were composed in roughly equal numbers of the foot regiments which formed part of Essex's own army and the five regiments of the London Trained Band. Essex's infantry consisted of thirteen regiments, all (with the possible exception of his own regiment of foot) very much below strength, perhaps averaging about 400 men apiece. These were organised into four brigades, each of three regiments, with Essex's own regiment and Sir William Springate's Regiment of Foot forming independent units.

The Londoners formed a separate brigade, though in practice its strong regiments, averaging about 900 men apiece, were employed independently.

The organisation of the horse, about 6,000 strong, is more obscure. Elements of nine regiments plus Essex's Lifeguard were present, so that the average unit was probably reasonably well up to strength with about 500 troopers. They were formed into two separate wings, the larger one led by Sir Philip Stapleton and the smaller one under John Middleton. There is some evidence that they may have been subdivided into three or more brigades.

Essex began forming up his troops at or just before dawn (about 5.30 a.m.). On the far left of his line, at the edge of the water meadows of the River Kennet in a heavily enclosed area east of the village of Enbourne, was stationed Lord Robartes' brigade of foot, consisting of his own regiment together with those of Sir William Constable and Colonel Martin, about 1,200 men in all. Acting as a 'forlorn hope' and lining the hedges of a number of small enclosures was a detachment of musketeers under Lieutenant-Colonel Fortescue. Robartes was a West Country magnate with little military experience but significant political influence, who served with Essex's army without particular distinction for much of the war. On this occasion he was supported and flanked by what was in effect a brigade of horse under Colonel Middleton, quite possibly consisting of his own, Lord Gray's and Denbigh's regiments, which had regularly served together through the course of the campaign and which may have totalled in the region of 1,400 men.

To the right of Robartes was stationed the red-coated full-time London regiment of Randell Mainwaring, which was part of the London Brigade. To its right was Philip Skippon's brigade, formed from his own, Sir William Brookes' and Henry Bulstrode's regiments. This entire wing of the army was under the overall command of Philip Skippon.

There was apparently initially a gap on Skippon's right, then came Harry Barclay's brigade, again consisting of three regiments: his own, John Holmestead's and Thomas Tyrell's (formerly John Hampden's) regiments. This brigade eventually formed approximately along the line of Bigg's Hill Lane.

The first line of Parliamentarian foot was completed by James Holbourne's Brigade, formed from his own, Francis Thompson's and George Langham's regiments. To the rear and on the right flank of Barclay and Holbourne were the remainder of the Parliamentarian horse, about 3,000 men, under Sir Philip Stapleton.

The London Brigade, consisting of the Red and Blue Regiments and the Blue, Red and Orange Auxiliaries, perhaps under Colonel Edmund Harvey, and possibly together with the Earl of Essex's foot regiment, were originally stationed in reserve behind the centre of the approximately 2-mile-long Parliamentarian line, near the artillery and train in Hamstead Park.[7] Harvey's London regiment of horse was certainly present with the army, although Skippon in practice exercised close personal control.

The somewhat piecemeal deployment of the Parliamentarian forces evolved as a result of the unexpected opportunities which now presented themselves because of the Royalist neglect of the previous evening. The tenor of Essex's address to his troops, no doubt composed during the hours of darkness, suggested that he expected dawn to bring the unwelcome spectacle of Royalist forces present in strength on the commanding high ground to the west of Newbury, and it must have come as a welcome surprise to the Parliamentarian commanders to discover that this was not the case. They had quickly appreciated the significance of the high ground around Biggs and Round Hills, and 'by break of day' (probably by about 6 a.m.):

> ...order was given for our march to an hill called Bigs-hill neere Newbury, and the onely convenient place for us to gaine, that we might with better security force our passage.[8]

Essex realised that the key high ground east of Skinner's Green was for the moment held by no more than a few Royalist cavalry patrols. Possibly urged on by Skippon, he was quick to seize the opportunity:

> ...when His Excellency perceived that the enemies' forces had possest themselves of that hill [Bigg's Hill] marching himself upon the head of his own Regiment, Colonel Barclay's [Brigade] and Colonel Holbourne's [Brigade] he charged so fiercely, that he beat them from the hill...[9]

In reality the Royalist cavalry probably fell back making little or no resistance, and Essex was able to extend his line to the south, pushing out Barclay and Holbourne's foot along the hedges on the line of Bigg's Hill Lane, with Stapleton's horse coming up in support and on their right.

At the same time Philip Skippon's Brigade, encountering equally light resistance, moved up Skinner's Green Lane to occupy Round Hill. Daylight thus presented the Royalists with an unpleasant surprise. Far from disappearing during the course of the night, their opponents were now occupying a position of advantage, and in effect forcing the Cavaliers to take the offensive. As related by what may be called the Royalist 'official' account, the Parliamentarians had placed baggage and reserve:

> Upon a Hill side under a Wood neer Hampstead, fenced by hedges and ditches inaccessible but by such and such passes, and having disposed another principal part of their strength betwixt it and a place called Enbourne, in strong hedges and houses, with apt Batteries on both sides, for bravadoes sake, or to invite us, they had drawn out into Battalia, into a little Heath [Enbourne Heath] on the South side of Enbourne three bodies of Foot, both lined and flanked with strong bodies of Horse and under favour of Cannon, so as that upon all occasions they might conveniently pour out of their Holds what new strength they pleased, or, if beaten, might have a safe Retreat, into the adjoining Fastnesses.[10]

The writer admitted that it might have appeared a wiser course of action for the Royalists to take advantage of their relatively secure supply lines and their possession of the town of Newbury in order to stand on the defensive and starve the enemy out. But:

> ...the answer to this objection, by way of excuse, [is] that we were in some sort so lead on, and ingaged by the tempting prospect of that little Batttalia I mentioned upon the Heath, and by way of justification I am to tell you, that there was within the Enemies' Domination a round hill not suspected or observed by us the night before from whence a battery would command all the plain before Newbury, where the King's Army stood, insomuch that unless we possesst ourselves of that hill, there was no holding of that field, but the King must have retreated with all his Army thence...[11]

It was also claimed that the King was persuaded to take the offensive by over-confident courtiers and junior officers, and that the battle was forced on him as a result of premature and ill-coordinated attacks by subordinates. However, while it is true that, based on their experience earlier in the campaign, the Royalists had reason to regard their cavalry as superior to that of Essex, they had so far made little impression on his foot, and could have no real grounds for supposing that they would be any easier a prospect when holding such a strong defensive position. The 'official' explanation of the King's decision to attack is undoubtedly the correct one. Despite the evident difficulties which it would involve, he would have little prospect of victory unless he could force the Parliamentarians from the strong positions which they had occupied on the high ground.

The Royalist deployment and plan of attack shows every sign of being hastily improvised. So far as numbers were concerned, the opposing armies were approximately equal. The Royalists however, had perhaps 2–3,000 more cavalry than their opponents, and some of these were of better quality. There seem to have been elements of at least thirty regiments present, indicating that some units were very much understrength. The organisation of the Royalist horse on the day is not entirely clear, but they seem to have been formed into at least five brigades. The approximately 8,000 foot were drawn from about twenty-five regiments, suggesting an average strength of no more than 300 men. They were probably formed into four brigades, together with a detached body of 'commanded' musketeers.

Skippon had joined Essex on the summit of Round Hill, from which point they saw 'a great strength of the enemy both horse and foot, in divers great bodies, advancing directly towards the way [Skinner's Green Lane] which all of our train was of necessity to march'.

The Royalists deployed hastily, probably more or less in reaction to the enemy moves, and planned in general terms two major and two subsidiary attacks on the Parliamentarian positions.

On the far right of the King's position, an advance was to be made through the water meadows of the Kennet towards Enbourne by troops commanded by Sir William Vavasour, Colonel-General of Gloucestershire. Vavasour was a professional soldier who had served in Europe until 1639, and who in the spring of 1643 had been sent to revitalise the sagging Royalist war effort in South Wales and its borders.

Vavasour himself was an experienced and at least acceptably competent officer, but the troops under his command, probably made up almost entirely of infantry, were not. They consisted of a mixture of troops raised in the first half of 1643 in Worcestershire and Gloucestershire, including

Vavasour's own regiment and that of Samuel Sandys. These had been formed into a brigade or 'tertia' by the addition of three regiments from South Wales. These, the regiments of Sir Anthony Mansell, Richard Bassett and Richard Donnell, were Trained Band units which had been forcibly called out by the local Royalist magnate, the Marquis of Worcester, and sent to join the King's forces at the siege of Gloucester. They lacked training, commitment and, possibly, adequate equipment. In all, Vavasour's brigade may have totalled about 1,500 men. They were supported by a few horse, probably Vavasour's own small unit, and eventually by the two troops of the King's Lifeguard of Horse, which seems initially to have been in reserve.

Next in line, faced with the tough objective of Round Hill, was the infantry brigade commanded by Sir Nicholas Byron. Byron was another experienced professional soldier, described as 'a person of great affability and dexterity, as well as martial knowledge.'[12] He had served in the Scots Wars and had led a foot tertia with some success at the Battle of Edgehill.

In theory at least, the six regiments under Byron's command included some of the best of the Royalist foot. Among them were five regiments of the Oxford Army, including the King's Lifeguard of Foot and the Lord General's, Thomas Blagge's, Charles Gerard's, Sir Lewis Dyve's and Lord Grandison's regiments. Some of these had been in existence since the start of the war, and in most cases had not been involved in the heavy losses incurred in the storm of Bristol. Byron's remaining unit, the Prince of Wales Regiment of Foot, commanded by a veteran of the war in Ireland, Michael Woodhouse, was, with 700 men, among the strongest units in the Royalist army. Although many of its rank and file had been raised fairly recently along the Welsh border, some of the officers had seen service in Ireland, and the unit had already gained a fearsome reputation for brutality, notably at the capture of Hopton Castle in March[13] when a number of Parliamentarian prisoners had been brutally despatched after surrendering.

Byron's brigade was probably the strongest of the Royalist foot formations, perhaps with as many as 2,000 men. However, it remained to be seen how successful Byron's men, exhausted by their long march, would be in pressing home an attack against a determined enemy in a strong defensive position.

In recognition of the vital and difficult task which faced Byron, soon after the deployment began Prince Rupert detached a brigade of horse to support him. This was led by Nicholas's nephew, Sir John Byron. Described by Clarendon as 'a person of a very ancient family, an honourable extraction, good fortune, and as unblemished a reputation as any gentleman of England',[14] Byron, with previous military experience on the Continent, had been given command of the first regiment of horse to be raised in 1642 and had proved himself an outstanding cavalry commander, with a number of minor successes to his credit, and a leading role in the decisive victory at Roundway Down. Though prickly and somewhat quarrelsome in temperament, Byron possessed the kind of drive and stubborn determination which would be invaluable in the situation facing the Royalists at Newbury.

His brigade consisted of his own veteran regiment of horse, of perhaps 300 men, together with those of Sir Thomas Aston and Thomas Morgan, possibly about 600 men in all. Aston had so far had an 'unlucky war'. After fighting at Edgehill he had been sent back to his native Cheshire to take command there as Colonel-General, but was recalled to Oxford after suffering several reverses, caused in part by lack of support from some of the local Royalists.

There is some uncertainty regarding the deployment of the remaining Royalist foot, but occupying the centre of their 'start line' were most of the rest of the King's infantry, although it is difficult to be sure of their exact positions.

They seem to have been organised into two more infantry brigades, together with the detached body of 'commanded' musketeers. One brigade was commanded by Colonel John Belasyse. A Roman Catholic from Yorkshire, Belasyse had first led a brigade of foot at Edgehill and had distinguished himself in the storming of Bristol, where he had been wounded. His brigade consisted of his own regiment, together with a number of other units of the Oxford Army foot. They included the regiments of Richard Bolle, Sir Ralph Dutton, John Owen and Lord Rivers. The brigade probably totalled about 1,500 men.

The remaining foot tertia known to have been present was led by Sir Gilbert Gerard, a Lancashire man who had fought at Edgehill and Bristol. His brigade seems to have consisted of a mixture of Welsh and northern units, some of which were very weak and brigaded together. They included his own regiment and those of Lord Molyneux and Sir Thomas Tyldesley from Lancashire. Neither of the latter are likely to have mustered more than 200 men apiece. Also with Gerard were the Welsh regiments of John Stradling, Sir Charles Lloyd, Richard Herbert and Anthony Thelwall. He also probably led the infantry, originally detachments from the Earl of Newcastle's army, which had escorted supplies of munitions south to Oxford in the spring. These included elements of units commanded by Conyers D'Arcy, William Eure, Thomas Blackwell, Thomas Pinchbeck and the small regiment of Lord Percy. These weak units were probably brigaded together into one or more larger formations. In all they may have totalled about 2,000 men.

Also present, and seeing action at various times at the northern edge of Wash Common and against Round Hill, was a detachment of 'commanded' musketeers. Lieutenant-Colonel George Lisle had earlier led this strong force, 1,000 strong, drawn mainly from regiments in the Bristol garrison. Lisle was a professional soldier of widely recognised ability, who had served at Edgehill and Chalgrove. For some reason, at Newbury he seems to have served under a more senior officer, Lord Thomas Wentworth. The role of the commanded musketeers was likely to be an important one. In the kind of 'hedge fight' which seemed likely to take place, pikemen would be of limited value, and a mobile force of musketeers which could be committed to add weight to an attack as required might prove invaluable.

The bulk of the horse were deployed at the southern end of the Royalist line, on and around Wash Common. Once again it is difficult to be certain of the details of their organisation. Rupert was of course in overall command, with Wilmot as his second, though how they divided responsibility between them on the day is unclear. In addition to Byron's, there seem to have been at least four brigades of horse: Rupert's own, presumably led by a senior colonel, Lord Wilmot's, Sir Charles Gerard's and the Earl of Carnarvon's. Both Gerard and Carnarvon were highly experienced in their roles. Gerard had been a professional soldier in Europe and was a close ally of Rupert, while the chivalrous and popular Carnarvon had served ably in the west during the early summer.

Each brigade probably averaged about 1,500 troopers, organised into three divisions of 500 men each. This will have involved brigading together some weaker regiments, though it is impossible to be certain of the composition of each brigade.

Also perhaps serving with the cavalry, in the role of dismounted musketeers and in order to give them increased fire support, were those Royalist dragoons present, who probably included Prince Rupert's Regiment and that of Colonel Henry Washington.

The lighter artillery pieces were probably deployed in support of the infantry formations, although the King certainly established at least one battery of heavier guns near the site of the tumuli on Wash Common, where they could fire on the Parliamentarian centre.

In the sort of improvised close-quarter fighting which characterised the action at Newbury, often with quite long intervals between successive attacks, it is likely that the disposition of troops on both sides was altered on a number of occasions during the day. In the case of the Royalists this may have happened several times. This reflects the haste with which the discomfited Cavaliers had to make their plans on the morning of 20 September, preparing for a battle in which, quite unexpectedly, but entirely as result of their own failings of the previous evening, they were now at a distinct disadvantage.

6

Newbury
The Battle

It is virtually impossible to be certain of the exact order of events in what was an exceptionally confused battle even by the standards of the English Civil War. Fighting extended for a period of over twelve hours, until finally brought to an end by the onset of darkness. It must have included quite considerable, though unrecorded, lulls, and periods when the main activity consisted of varyingly effective exchanges of artillery fire. Fighting seems to have flared up and then died down again on different sectors of the front, with little if any coordination between them. However such evidence as exists suggests that serious fighting began first on the wings of both armies, with the attacks by Vavasour in the Kennet water-meadows and Rupert on Wash Common beginning the battle. For the sake of completeness these will be described first, before examining the fiercest and arguably most important fighting which took place in the centre. But it should be remembered that, for much of the time, fighting of some sort was taking place in all of these sectors more or less simultaneously.

It was probably around 7 a.m. that the first shots of the battle were fired. Skippon was back with the reserve consisting of the London Brigade, and had begun the process of sending forward individual units together with guns from the Train. According to Henry Foster, the men of the Red Regiment began the day with 'most cheerfull and courageous spirits'[1]. As fighting began on the southern fringes of the Kennet water-meadows, Foster and his comrades were ordered by Skippon to take up position on Robartes' right flank, on the slopes of Round Hill. As Foster remembered:

> The Lord Robert's soldiers had begun to skirmish with them before we came up to the enemy: which we hearing, put us to a running march till we sweat again, hastening to their relief and succour.[2]

According to the most detailed Parliamentarian version of events:

> That Forlorn-hope which he [Skippon] had commanded the night before being now strengthened with 300 musketeers, and led by Major [Richard] Fortescue,

Major-General Skippon placed on the left of my Lord Roberts his brigade; upon the high way that came from Newbury just upon us, [the Newbury–Enborne road] upon which way 4 Drakes were likewise placed, and well defended; though the Enemies came up so close, that they took away a limmer [limber] of one of our peeces, but it was with losse of many of their lives.[3]

Lord Robartes' Brigade also came under attack, although here the assault was evidently pressed less closely. Skippon had deployed Robartes:

...with foure or five smalle pieces just where the Enemie advanced, who gave them so warme an entertainment that they ran shamefully; and my Lord Roberts possessed the ground which the Enemy came first up unto: his Lieutenant-Colonel was shott in the face...[4]

Royalist accounts of the action in this sector are sparse, but it certainly does not appear that the attack was pressed home with any vigour or that it continued for very long. It may be that it was never intended as more than a diversionary action to pin down Parliamentarian reserves, but in any case Vavasour's troops were unlikely to present a serious threat. When Vavasour had joined the King in August he had brought with him 300 horse and 1,200 foot, the majority of them pikemen, commanded by Colonel Herbert Price. Although they had later been reinforced by the High Sheriff of Glamorgan, Sir Richard Bassett, with an additional 500-strong regiment based on the Glamorgan Trained Bands, there is no evidence that the ratio of musketeers to pikes was greatly increased. In the fighting in the enclosures outside Enbourne, as elsewhere on the field, pikemen would have been virtually useless, and Vavasour almost certainly had too few musketeers to make any progress. The terrain was so enclosed that both Colonel Middleton's Parliamentarian horse and Vavasour's small detachment of cavalry were of little use and 'could not be engaged but in small parties by reason of the hedges.'[5]

The counter-attack mounted by Lord Robartes seems quickly to have ground to a halt, checked by the intervention of the King's Lifeguard of Horse and possibly by Vavasour's small cavalry force, which were probably in reserve. This seems to have been the end of any fighting of note in this sector. Casualties in Vavasour's tertia are known to have included two captains, one ensign and seventy-eight common soldiers, the proportions of dead and wounded being unclear.[6]

If fighting on the northern part of the battlefield was relatively low-key and probably of fairly short duration, the encounter at the southern end of the field on Wash and Enbourne Commons was very different. Prince Rupert had deployed in the region of 6,000 horse on the Wash Common, and hoped to take advantage of the Royalist superiority in this arm and the relatively open ground to smash the Parliamentarian horse and then swing right to attack the enemy foot in the centre.

As they had to, if they were to achieve their aim, the Royalists took the initiative. Once again the Parliamentarians provide the most detailed account:

> Sir Ph: Stapleton with his Exc. Guard and Regiment of horse advanced upon the plaine of the hill, when he had no sooner drawne up out of the Lanes and seconded by Col: Dalbier's Reg: of horse (no other horse being then advanced to the place) but the Enemy, perceiving this advantage, being all drawne already in severall great bodies of horse, part of them advanced immediately, and charged our horse, whom we so well received, (giving no fire till we joined close with them) that the Enemy was wholly routed, and pursued with much execution neer to the place where their whole body of horse stood.[7]

It is interesting to note from this account signs of a modification of the tactics previously employed by the Parliamentarian horse. Although they evidently still remained stationary to receive the enemy charge, they were now increasing the effectiveness of their fire by reserving it until the last moment in a similar fashion to the Royalists.

Stapleton's horse had won the first round, but they had so far only been engaged with a small part (possibly one brigade) of the Royalist cavalry, and fierce fighting lay ahead. Seeing the enemy strength, the Parliamentarian horse:

> ...by order...drew back to our first ground, by occasion whereof opportunity was gained to bring up the remainder of our horse which had the rearguard that day, viz: Sir James Ramsay, Col: Godwin, Col: Harvey, Col: Norton, and the three commanded troops under Sir Samuel Luke, whereupon the Enemy drew out some fresh Regiments of his horse, and with all possible haste advanced againe upon Sir Philip, but received no better entertainment than before, being againe routed by him. By that time that he had drawne up his Regiment againe into some order, the other Regiments, Ramsey, Harvey, Goodwin) were coming up to him, where the Enemy with their whole Body charged upon them bravely, and were as well received. Sir Philip Stapleton was here charged front and flank, his whole Regiment having spent both their Pistols, and were so encompassed, that the Enemy and ours, with both our whole bodies, were all mixed together, and in this confusion

many were slaine on both sides, and our men at last were forced towards the lanes end [Bigg's Hill Lane] where they first came in. Which being neer our Foot, the Enemie endeavoured to disengage, themselves, and drew back to their own forces. Those that entered the lane with ours were most of them slaine. We took three colours of horse compleat, and a peece of another coloure; one of the colours which we took, was the Harp with the Crown Royall, the Motto 'Lyrica Monarchica'; another, having an Angell with a flaming sword treading on a Dragon, the motto 'Quis ut Deus': a third with a French motto 'Courage Pour la Cause'. In the first charge Col: Dalbier and Commissary Copley charging with much bravery were both wounded. In the third charge Capt; Hamond, Cap: Fleetwood, Cap: Pym, and Cornet Doyley were all wounded. Cap: Draper who led the the forlorn hope of Sir Philip Stapleton's men, behaved himself very gallantly, as Cap: Abercromby, and Cap: Shibborne did with the Dragooners...[8]

The Royalists seem to have been halted in Skinner's Green Lane largely by a counter-attack by Captain Draper and by the accurate fire of the two companies of dragoons.

It is unfortunate that no detailed Royalist account of what was obviously a very fiercely contested action appears to survive, but it is clear that, as might be expected, Prince Rupert was in the thick of the action, at least in its later stages. The Parliamentarian Bulstrode Whitlocke related how:

Sir Philip Stapleton (though he would not acknowledge it) that being with other Parliament Commanders in the head of a body of horse facing another body of the King's horse, before whom stood their commanders, and the chief of them was Prince Rupert. The Parliament Officer desiring to cope singly with the Prince, he rode from before his company up to the body of horse, before whom the Prince with divers other Commanders were, and had his pistol in his hand ready cockt and fitted. Coming up to them alone, he looked one and another of them in the face, and when he came to Prince Rupert, whom he knew, he fired his pistol in the Prince's face, but his armour defended him from any hurt, and having done this, he turned his horse about, and came gently off again without any hurt, though many pistols were fired at him... Another passage was of Sir Philip Stapleton's groom, a Yorkshire man, and stout, if not too rash. By this story, he was attending on his master in a charge, where the groom's mare was killed under him, but he came off on foot back again to his own company. To some of whom he complained that he had forgotten to take off his saddle and bridle from his mare, and to bring them away with him; and said that they were a new saddle and bridle, and that the cavaliers should not get so much by him, but he would go again and fetch them: his master and friends persuaded him not to adventure in so rash an act, the mare lying dead close to the enemy who would mall him, if he came so near them, and his master promised to give him another new saddle and bridle. But this would not persuade the groom to leave his saddle and bridle to the cavaliers, but he went again to fetch them, and stayed to pull off the saddle and bridle, while hundreds of bullets flew about his ears, and brought them back with him, and had no hurt at all...[9]

Less fortunate was that excellent Royalist cavalry officer, the Earl of Carnarvon, who after the rout of one of the Parliamentarian attacks:

...coming carelessly back by some of the scattered troopers, was by one of them, who knew him, run through the body with a sword, of which he died within an hour.[10]

It is unclear how long the cavalry encounter on Wash Common went on, but significant casualties must have resulted for both sides. It was certainly the toughest fight which Rupert's horse had so far experienced, with their opponents performing much more creditably than in previous engagements. However the Parliamentarian cavalry had now been driven back behind the line of Bigg's Hill Lane, where they made a stand, but seem to have played no further part in the battle. Once reorganised, the Royalist horse were now in a position to attack the right flank of the Parliamentarian centre, where their assistance was sorely needed.

After sending the Red Auxiliary Regiment to support Lord Robartes in the Kennet valley, Skippon still had four London foot regiments, together with some artillery, in reserve. They would soon be in action.

The Royalists were keenly aware of the significance of the high ground centred on Round Hill and directed their main efforts to capturing it. The first attack, probably soon after 6.30 a.m., was spearheaded by the 'commanded' musketeers of Thomas Wentworth and George Lisle, backed by horse. The Royalists were firmly confronted by the foot of Skippon's brigade, amidst a network of thickly-hedged small enclosures. The initial advance seems to have been supported by a weak brigade, or commanded party, of horse, which may have been led by Sir Charles Lucas, an experienced professional soldier. Lucas (if indeed he was the author of this anonymous account) describes how he:

...drew the partye of horse into a close that contained a considerable part of the hill, [probably Round Hill] then we discovered the enemy, and there began the service. But before reliefe could come to the musketeers, they retreated, and I drew the horse into the next close, though not without losse both with great and small shott where we stood, until in which time my horse received a shott in his neere shoulder. But the foot crying out for the horse, I returned into the first mentioned close and was very slowly followed [by his troopers] by reason of the straitness of the passage, and when I thought I had men enough to doe the service, I went to the furthest part of the said close where were neere about 1,000 of the enemies foote drawne up in order and one piece of artillery, and as I was charging my horse was shott againe in the breast and faltered with me, for that, I being out of hopes to do other service than to lose myself, I gave orders to the party in these very words in Major [Paul] Smith's hearing – 'Fall on, my Masters! For I must go change my horse.' And in my coming I met with my Lord Byron. My distresse at that time compelled me to desire him to lend mee a horse. I likewise desired the same favour of Sir Lewis Kirke, but presently meeting with Sergeant-Major Daniel, major to the Prince of Wales his regiment, hee lent mee a horse. That horse I changed for one of Captain Sheldon's of His Highness Prince Maurice his regiment, which I conceived to be much better. When I was thus supplied I was going back to my charge, which I thought Major Smith would have had a care of in my absence, as I had conceived in duty he ought, I being for that present disabled, but in my way back contrary to my expectation I found Captain Scot of Sir Arthur Aston's regiment and Capt. Panton of Lord Carnarvon's regiment, and some other officers of the party with about 40 men. I desired that wee might goe up the Hill again, Captain Panton answered mee that my Lord Lieutenant General [Wilmot] commanded them to stay in that same place, whereupon I sent one to him to know his further commands. In the meantime came Sir Lewis Kirke to mee with commands from the King to goe looke to the passé by the river side which the enemy were then endeavouring to gaine, but when I came to the place I found Sir William Vavasour there with his brigade, which I conceived sufficiently secured that place. Whereupon I sent Captain Scot to His Majesty that I might goe to some place where I might doe him better service, which His Majesty did not grant.[11]

It seems from his account that this Royalist officer, after his horse was shot, had made his way back to the northern edge of Wash Common and Enbourne Heath, where he encountered some of the right wing of Rupert's horse fresh from defeating Stapleton. It is also apparent that the cavalry under his command had found attacking into the enclosed terrain where the Parliamentarians were stationed a daunting prospect, and that without their support the 'commanded' musketeers had also faltered. This impression is confirmed by Sir John Byron, who was coming into action on the eastern slopes of Round Hill:

> ...about 5 in the morning [probably in fact about an hour later] I had orders to march towards a little hill full of enclosures, which the enemy (through the negligence before mentioned) had possessed himself of and had brought up two small field pieces and was bringing up more, whereby they would both have secured their march on Reading (the highway was lying hard by) and withal so annoyed our army which was drawn up in the bottom, where the King himself was, that it would have been impossible for us to have kept the ground. The hill, as I mentioned, was full of enclosures and extremely difficult for horse service, so that my orders were, only with my own and Sir Thos Aston's regiment to draw behind the commanded foot led by Lord Wentworth and Col. George Lisle, and to be ready to second them, in case the enemy's horse should advance towards them: the rest of my brigade was by Prince Rupert commanded to the Heath, where most of the other horse and foot were drawn.[12]

The Royalist 'commanded' musketeers found themselves hotly engaged among the hedgerows by Skippon's brigade, and the attack quickly bogged down as the Cavaliers went to ground behind the cover of the hedges and high lane-side banks. Sir Nicholas Byron's strong tertia of Oxford Army foot was ordered up in their support, and his nephew, Sir John, once more takes up the story:

> The commanded foot not being able to make good the place, my uncle Byron, who commanded the first tertia, instantly came up with part of the regiment of guards and Sir Michael Woodhouse's and my Lord Gerard's regiments of foot [Gerard's], commanded by his Lieutenant-Colonel, Ned Villiers, but the service grew so hot, that in a very short time, of twelve ensigns that marched up with my Lord Gerard's regiment, eleven were brought off the field hurt, and Ned Villiers shot through the shoulder. Upon this a confusion was heard among the foot, calling horse! horse! whereupon I advanced with those two regiments I had, and commanded them to halt while I went to view the ground, and to see what way there was to that place where the enemy's foot were drawn up, which I found to be enclosed with a high quick hedge and no passage into it, but by a narrow gap through

which but one horse at a time could go and that not without difficulty.. My lord of Falkland did me the honour to ride in my troop this day, and I would needs go along with him, the enemy had beat our foot out of the close, and was drawne up near the hedge; I went to view, and as I was giving orders for making the gap wide enough, my horse was shott in the throat with a musket bullet and his bit broken in his mouth so that I was forced to call for another horse, in the meantime my Lord Falkland (more gallantly than advisedly) spurred his horse through the gap, where he and his horse were immediately killed...[13]

Particularly during Victorian times, the death of Falkland was regarded as the most celebrated incident of the battle. Before the war Falkland had enjoyed a wide reputation as an intellectual and a moderate Royalist, who had opposed excesses of monarchical power. He had become a Secretary of State in January 1642, but, although he fought in the ranks of the Royalist cavalry at Edgehill in much the same way as he did at Newbury, he became increasingly despondent at the deepening bitterness of the prolonged conflict. His opposition to the war was well known, and he wrote to his friend Edward Hyde just before the battle of Newbury that:

...so much notice had been taken of him for an impatient desire of peace that it was necessary he should make it appear that it was not out of fear of the utmost hazard of war...[14]

However the seventeenth-century antiquary John Aubrey suggested a less idealistic motivation:

Anno domini 1643 at the fight at Newbury, my Lord Falkland being there, and having nothing to do decided to charge; as the two armies were engaging, rode in like a madman (as he was) between them, and was (as he needs must be) shot. Some that were your superfine discoursing politicians and fine gentlemen, would needs have the reason for this mad action of throwing away his life so, to be his discontent for the unfortunate advice given to his Master as aforesaid; [to besiege Gloucester] but I have been well informed, by those that best knew him, and knew the intrigues behind the curtain (as they say) that it was the grief of the death of Mrs Moray, a handsome lady at Court, who was his mistress, and whom he loved above all creatures, was the cause of his being so madly guilty of his own death, as aforementioned...[15]

A disregard for danger, possibly resulting from one or both of the suggested motives, was almost certainly the real cause of Falkland's death, rather than an overt suicide bid. Falkland probably rode out into a narrow track then known as Dark Lane, which no longer exists, and was shot down by enemy musketeers in the hedges on either side.

To return to Byron's activities:

> The passage being then made somewhat wide, and I not having another horse, drew in my own troop first, giving orders for the rest to follow, and charged the enemy, who entertained us with a great salvo of musket shott, and discharged their two drakes upon us, laden with case shott, which killed some and hurt many of my men, so that we were forced to wheel off and could not meet them at that charge. I rallied my men together again, but not so soon but that the enemy had got away their field pieces for fear of the worst, seeing us resolved not to give over, so I charged them a second time, Sir Thomas Aston being then come up with his regiment, we then beat them at the end of the close, where they faced us again, having the advantage of a hedge at their backs, and poured in another volley of shott upon us, when Sir Thomas Aston's horse was killed under him, and withal kept us off so with their pikes we could not break them, but were forced to wheel off again, they in the meantime retreating into another little close and making haste to recover a lane which was very near unto it [Skinner's Green Lane] finding then they could keep the ground, which before they could do, I rallied the horse again, and charged them a third time, and then utterly routed them, and had not left a man of them unkilled, but that the hedges were so high the horse could not pursue them, and besides a great body of their own foot advanced toward the lane to relieve them. Our foot then drew upon the ground from whence we had beaten the enemy, and kept it, and [I] drew the horse back to the former station; for upon this service I lost near upon a hundred horse and men out of my regiment, whereof out of my own troop twenty-six. The enemy drew up fresh supplies to regain the ground again, but [due] to my uncle's good conduct (who that day did extraordinary service) was entirely beaten off...[16]

The fight for Round Hill was one of the most hotly contested actions of the battle, and represented a remarkable achievement for Byron's cavalry. They had encountered well-trained and motivated opponents, whose musketeers had made good use of the cover of the hedgerows before rallying in a hedgehog formation under the protection of their pikes, their rear protected from attack by another hedge, and then making a further fighting retreat. Despite this, and sustaining losses which in the case of Byron's regiment probably amounted to a third of its strength, the Royalist horse had succeeded in taking a significant part of Round Hill.

It seems clear that the close-quarter fighting was particularly savage. It was not unusual when horse attacked bodies of foot with the determination displayed by Byron and Aston's men for riders to be dragged from their mounts when they attempted to penetrate enemy ranks and summarily despatched. Among the colours captured by the Parliamentarians at Newbury were three bearing ass's heads, possibly a pun on the name 'Aston', and belonging to his regiment. It is quite likely that at least one of their bearers fell in the manner described.

Unsurprisingly the Royalist newspaper, *Mercurius Aulicus*, emphasised this incident of an otherwise disappointing day for the Royalists. It is clear that Byron's account somewhat telescopes the sequence of events:

> Many of their [the Parliamentarians'] living have cause to remember how the little enclosed hill commanding the town of Newbury, and the plaine, where His Majesty in person was drawne up (being the first place attempted by our foot by daybreak) was then prepossessed by a great body of their foot, till in their advance of it, ours beate them off into the hedgerows, under which shelter they much annoyed both our foot and horse, the right valiant L-Col. Villiers and ten of his ensigns being hurt upon the ground the rebels first stood on, yet though they lost the hill, they kept the hedges all the forenoon, till a fresh supply of neare 200 musqueteers advancing up a lane [Dark Lane?] to surprise our pikes and colours [which were stationed in the rear] by that gallant and resolute charge made by Sir Thos. Aston with his own troope (through a double-quick hedge) those poachers were dislodged, their fresh supply routed, and fled before him in such haste, that though his horse was shot in the entrance to the lane and drew him by the leg among them, they had not the civility to help him up, but let him walk away on foot leaving their pykes and colours to shift for themselves, and never again regained the place. But Prince Rupert himselfe drew down a fresh relief of foot and made good the lane against them, and about three of the clock two small pieces of ours being then drawn up to that hill, which was the place of most concernment, and was never quit by us till the King drew off all his foot in a body to Newbury field, nor ever after manned by them...[17]

Parliamentarian accounts of this phase of the action are unfortunately much briefer. It seems likely that the counter-attack which Sir John Byron describes being mounted against Sir Nicholas Byron late in the day was made by reinforcements brought up from the reserve by Skippon, and is probably the action described in this Parliamentarian account:

> The Major General [Skippon] rode up to the top of the hill, where he espied an advantage to bestow 8 or 10 Demiculvering shot upon the Enemy, who out of an house pelted the forenamed gentlemen at neer-distance; then he rallied the two Train-Band Regiments [the Red and Blue Regiments] into one Body, drew them up, and placed them before, where the train of artillery did afterwards draw up to the top of the hill [most probably at the end of Skinner's Green Lane], and desired Major Boteler [Earl of Essex's Regiment of Foot] to draw the Musquetiers of his Regiment on the right hand before the two Demi-Culverings, that were placed at the end of the Lane on the top of the hill, and the Red Auxiliaries he placed on the left hand of those peeces which before were slenderly guarded.... While this was acting, two peeces which belonged to the Major-General's Regiment, and one drake of Sir William Brooks were by his Excell: Regiment under the command of Major Boteler, with the assistance of 200 Musquetiers, recovered...[18]

There can be no doubt that the action for Round Hill was the most fiercely contested infantry engagement of the battle, nor that Nicholas Byron's Brigade suffered the bulk of the casualties inflicted on the Royalist foot. Known casualties, killed and wounded, include:

> The King's Lifeguard of Foot: 29 common soldiers
> Prince of Wales Regiment: 69 common soldiers, 2 Captains, 2 Lieutenants, 1 Ensign, 1 sergeant
> Lord Grandison's Regiment: 5 common soldiers wounded, 11 men killed
> Charles Gerard's Regiment: the Lieutenant-Colonel, 2 Captains, 2 Lieutenants, 9 Ensigns, 7 Sergeants, 78 common soldiers
> The Lord General's Regiment: 74 common soldiers.[19]

With at least 300 casualties out of a likely effective strength of about 2,000, Sir Nicholas Byron and his men had put up a creditable performance. The same, however, was not generally felt to be the case so far as the remainder of the King's foot were concerned. While Byron moved against Round Hill, the intention was that John Belasyse's and Sir Gilbert Gerard's brigades should attack on his left. They were to direct their assault on the Earl of Essex's Regiment of Foot and the brigades of Holbourne and Barclay, who were holding a position roughly following the line of Skinner's Green Lane at the northern end of Wash Common, where it was traversed by what was then known as Monkey Lane, the road to Reading.

Although the exact chronology of events is, as ever, confused, it seems that the Royalists may not have launched a major attack in this sector until late in the afternoon, perhaps at about 4 p.m., when the cavalry engagement on Wash Common was at an end and Rupert was able to spare some horse to support the infantry.

Sir John Byron was scathing about the performance of Belasyse's and Gilbert Gerard's men:

> What was done upon the Heath (where the main body of our horse and foot fought) I will not relate, because I was not an eye-witness of it, onely this is generally confest, that had not our foot play'd the poltroons extremely that day, we in all probability had set a period to the war...[20]

In the absence of any detailed account of events from their viewpoint, it is difficult to asses just how poor a performance was put up by the Royalist foot in this sector, or to speculate on possible reasons. The Royalists' 'official' version of events comments that 'our foot having found a hillock in the heath that sheltered them from the enemy's cannon, would not be drawn a foot from thence'.[21] This suggestion of half-heartedness by some at least of the Royalist infantry in this sector is supported by the recollections of Captain John Gwynne, serving with Charles Lloyd's regiment in Gilbert Gerard's brigade. He is possibly referring to an incident that took place quite early in the day:

> ...a wing of Essex his horse, moving gently towards us, made us leave our execution upon the enemy, and retreat into the next field, where were several gaps to get to it, but not direct in my way; yet, with the colours in my hand, I jumpt over hedge and ditch, or I had died by multitude of hands.[22]

A sporadic firefight, supported on the Royalist side by the guns of the main battery established on the eastern side of Wash Common, seems to have gone on for several hours in the late morning and early afternoon, but it was late in the day before the Royalists launched their main assault, directed against Essex's regiment and Barclay's and Holbourne's brigades. The Parliamentarians were evidently pushed back a short distance, but fortunately pressure further north had now eased sufficiently for Skippon to be able to redeploy Colonel Mainwaring's London foot regiment from its position on the slopes of Round Hill to assist in the threatened centre:

This regiment his Excellency a while after commanded away, to the relief of his own Regiment, Colonell Barckley's and Colonell Holbourne's Brigades which had been 4 hours upon very hot service. It fortuned that this Regiment was no sooner brought on, but they were overcharged with two great Bodies of horse and foot, so that they were forced to retreat, and lose that ground which the forenamed forces had gotten. Which Colonell Holbourne perceiving with his Brigade gave the enemy a Round Salvo, and instantly his own and Colonell Barckley's Brigades, and his Excell: Regiment again advancing Beat back the Enemy, gained the ground, and made good the place all the day after...[23]

The discomfiture of Mainwaring's regiment threatened to create a dangerous gap between Skippon's and Essex's wings of the Parliamentarian army, and the Royalist assault had been mounted with sufficient force to divert some of Butler's men from their counter-attack on Round Hill:

The Enemy drew away from their Pykes (which with their colours kept standing with many great bodies of Horse to guard them) 500 or 600 Musquetiers, besides Dragoons, to encompasse our men on the right hand among the hedges. Just at which time his Excell: sent to have 200 of the 300 musquetiers of the Forlorn hope to go to the relief of Col: Barclay's and Col; Holbourne's souldiers. But then the Enemy falling on our right hand diverted them, who with other of our Musquetiers thereabouts beat the Enemy off, who else had done us great mischief; this was about 4 a clock in the afternoon, when all our whole Army of foot was engaged in the fight; but then he also caused some of the red Auxiliary Regiment to draw nearer to Col: Barclay's post, as he himself required...[24]

The Royalist attack at the northern edge of Wash Common was apparently fairly serious, threatening both the right flank of the Parliamentarian centre and also its rear. Sergeant Foster relates the unpleasant situation in which he and his comrades found themselves as they were deployed onto open ground at the eastern end of Enbourne Heath in order to fill the gap in the Parliamentarian centre:

When we were come into the field, our two Regiments of the trained bands [Red and Blue] were placed in open Campania upon the right wing of the whole Army. The enemy had there planted 8 pieces of Ordnance, and stood in a great body of Horse and Foot, wee being placed right opposite against them, and far lesse than twice Musket shot distance from them. They began their

The First Battle of Newbury

battery against us with their great Guns, above halfe an hour before we could get any of our Guns up to us: our Gunner dealt very ill with us, delaying to come up to us, our noble Colonel Tucker fired one peece of Ordnance against the enemy, and aiming to give fire the second time, was shot in the head with a Cannon bullet from the enemy. The blew Regiment of the Trained Bands stood upon our right wing, and behaved themselves most gallantly. Two regiments of the King's Horse which stood upon their right flank afar off, came fiercely upon them, and charged them two or three times, but were beat back with their Musquetiers, who gave them a most desperate charge [volley], and made them flee. This day our whole Army wore green boughs in their hats, to distinguish us from our enemies; which they perceiving, one regiment of their Horse had got green boughs, and rid up to our regiments crying 'Friends, Friends', but we let flie at them, and made many of them and their horses tumble, making them flee with a vengeance. The enemies Canon did play most against the red Regiment of Trained Bands. They did some execution among us at the first, and were somewhat dreadfull when mens' bowels and brains flew in our faces. But blessed be God that gave us courage, so that we kept our ground, and after a while feared them not, our Ordnance did very good execution upon them, for we stood at so neere a distance upon a plain field, that we could not lightly misse one another. We were not much above halfe our Regiment in this place; for we had 60 Files of Musqutiers drawn off for the forlorne hope, who were ingaged again by the enemy in the field upon our left flank, where most of the Regiments of the Army were in fight. They had some small shelter of the hedges and bankes, yet had a very hot fight with the enemy, and did good execution, and stood to it as bravely as ever men did. When our two regiments of the Trained Bands had thus plaid against the enemy for the space of three hours, or thereabouts, our red Regiment joined to the Blew which stood a little distance from us, upon our left flank, where we gained the advantage of a little hill, which we maintained against the enemy halfe an hour: two Regiments of the enemies' foot fought against us all this while to gain the hill, but could not. Then two regiments of the enemies horse, which stood upon our right flank, came fiercely upon us, and so surrounded us, that wee were forced to charge [to form a defensive hedgehog, with pikes 'charged' to receive horse] upon them in the front and rear, and both Flanks, which was performed by us with a great deal of courage and undauntedness of spirit, insomuch that wee made a great slaughter among them, and forced them to retreat; but presently the two regiments of the enemies' foot in this time gained the hill, and came upon us before wee could well recover ourselves, that we were glad to retreat a little way into the field, till we had rallied up our men, and put them into their former posture, and then came on again...[25]

Foster's account suggests that a very hard fight indeed took place on the northern edge of Wash Common. The little hill to which he refers may be one of the tumuli situated in this area. The success of the Parliamentarian foot in repulsing the Royalist horse so effectively was remarkable, and speaks volumes both for their discipline and perhaps for the weariness of Rupert's horse after their tough encounter with Stapleton's men. It also seems to suggest that Byron's accusations regarding the poor performance of the Royalist foot here were exaggerated. The probability that they in fact performed at least adequately is borne out by known casualty figures:

John Belasyse's Brigade
Col. Bellasis' Regiment. 25: Col. Bowles [Richard Bolles] Regt., 23; Col. Dalton's [Sir Ralph Dutton] Regt., 22; Col: [John] Owen's Regt., 14; Col; Harford's [Richard Herbert] Regt., 13; Col. [Sir Lewis] Dyve's Regt., 14; Col. [Thomas] Blagge's Regt., 6 common soldiers.

Sir Gilbert Gerard's Brigade
9 officers slain, 22 shott, 100 soldiers slain, 116 shott[26]

The Parliamentarians regarded the action of the late afternoon in this area as the crisis of the battle. At one point the Royalist horse attacking the right flank of their foot seemed about to break through into the Parliamentarians' rear and fall on their baggage train. They saw the resistance put up by the Trained Bands, supported by a few horse, as being the key factor in frustrating the Royalists:

> Two regiments of the King's horse with a fierce charge, saluted the Blew Regiment of the London Trained Bands, who gallantly discharged upon them, and did beate them backe, but they being no whit daunted at it, wheeled about, and on a suddaine charged them againe. Our musketeers did againe discharge, and that with so much violence and successe that they sent them now, not wheeling but reeling from them, and yet for all that, they made a third assault, and coming in full squadrons, they did the utmost of their endeavours to breake through our ranks, but a cloud of bullets came at once so thick from our muskets, and made such a havocke among them, both of men and horse, that in a feare, full of confused speed, they did flye before us, and did no more adventure upon so warm a service.[27]

The Earl of Essex was himself hotly engaged in this part of the battle, his horse dying of exhaustion under him. As at Edgehill he proved happier in the role of a regimental officer fighting alongside his men than as commanding general, a role which seems largely to have been filled on the day by Philip Skippon, who himself wore out three horses in his ceaseless activity. Both Lord Robartes and Colonel Barclay were noted as providing steady leadership.

On the Royalist side King Charles, as might be expected, played no very active part in the fighting, probably remaining for much of the day near the Royalist start line just south of Newbury. Little is known of the activities of Lord Forth, or of the Major-General of Foot, Sir Jacob Astley. The nature of the battle and the piecemeal fashion in which the Royalist attacks were perforce delivered made Newbury very much a 'soldiers' battle'. The main responsibility for conducting it rested on brigade commanders, among whom the Byrons certainly played their part well, as evidently did Rupert and Wilmot. Of the remainder, lack of evidence prevents any clear judgement. Losses among the foot officers were particularly high, illustrating the nature of combat in which small parties of men were led forward, sometimes with difficulty, in savage little encounters among the lanes and hedgerows.

By about 7 p.m., with gathering dusk and possibly a resumption of the rain, fighting was dying down, although bursts of musket fire, as small parties and patrols clashed, continued well into the night. Around 10 p.m, possibly as much to clear their muskets and prevent their charges going damp over night as to make a gesture of defiance, the Royalist foot opposite Barclay's and Holbourne's brigades discharged their pieces in 'a round salvo' and then fell silent. With no clear idea of the outcome of the battle, the bulk of the exhausted men on both sides snatched what rest they could amid the dead and the groans of the wounded and dying and awaited, no doubt with keen anxiety, the dawn of the next day.

7
Aftermath

As darkness fell and fighting died down in the fields around Newbury, the commanders on both sides met to consider the outcome of the day and their next move. Both had apparently some grounds for satisfaction, but also pressing concerns.

For Essex and his commanders, the day had ended more favourably than they might have expected at the outset. They will have had no clear estimate of their casualties, and indeed an accurate figure remains difficult to calculate. The Red Regiment of the London Trained Bands, which had been in the thick of the action, had according to Henry Foster lost sixty or seventy dead, together with an unstated number of men wounded. Next morning Foster saw about 100 bodies, stripped naked during the night by looters, in the area of the Heath where fighting had been most intense. This might suggest a high overall total of casualties, but the Londoners had been fighting largely in the open and endured heavy artillery fire. Other foot regiments, fighting from behind the cover of hedges and banks, will not have suffered so severely. The horse also saw prolonged action, but in such engagements the majority of casualties were normally incurred in the pursuit if one side or the other broke in flight, and this did not happen at Newbury. Any attempt to reach a total must be largely guesswork, but a figure of about 1,200, including dead and seriously wounded, may be near to the mark.

The prompt action early in the morning inspired by Skippon had secured most of the key high ground to the west of Newbury and, with the exception of part of Round Hill, the Parliamentarians had succeeded in retaining much of it in the face of fierce attacks.

However, Essex and his Council of War will have been keenly aware that the Royalists remained between them and London. There was no sign of the support which they were optimistically hoping for from Sir William Waller, and supplies were running low. The situation as it appeared to them at the close of 20 September was summarised by a Parliamentarian account:

> ...the Enemy both horse and foot stood in good order on the further side of the Green, [Wash Common] where we expected their stay till next morning, and that they were working (as was reported) to place their Cannon, to

make use of them against us when day should break, against which supposed encounter we encouraged our souldiers beforehand, and resolved by God's help the next day to force our way through them or dye...[1]

Just how much enthusiasm the Parliamentarian commanders were able to instil into their men is open to question, for most of Essex's army spent a thoroughly miserable night. As well as enduring the inevitable rain, they were also lacking provisions of all kinds. Henry Foster remembered how:

...we were in great distress for water, or any accommodation to refresh our poor Souldiers... we were right glad to drink in the same water where our horses did drink, wandering up and down to seeke for it...[2]

All in all, despite their brave words, Essex and his officers must have been awaiting the morning with trepidation.

The Royalist Council of War would also review the events of the day with mixed feelings. They had been badly wrong-footed at the start of the battle, largely because of their own failure to reconnoitre the ground adequately on the evening of the 19th. As a result, Essex had beaten them to possession of most of the key positions and instead of being able to fight the defensive action which Rupert at least evidently would have preferred the Cavaliers had been forced to attack Essex on his chosen ground in a situation of considerable disadvantage to them.

The outcome had been disappointing, though not the disaster it might have been. Largely thanks to Rupert's cavalry, which had once again demonstrated their superiority (albeit diminishing), and to the fine performance by Sir John Byron's horse and some of his uncle's foot, the King's men had at least held their ground, although they had been unable to make any decisive advances.

Royalist casualties had also been heavy. Again exact figures are lacking, though we have a reasonable idea of those suffered among the foot. The list which survives among the papers of the Royalist Council of War gives a total of 588 officers and men killed, wounded or 'sick' after the battle.[3] This total does not include any casualties suffered by Wentworth and Lisle's 'commanded' musketeers, which possibly totalled something in the region of 100.

To these must be added the losses among the horse, which were evidently considerable. Both Rupert and Byron lost about 100 men out of their regiments and there were other significant casualties, particularly during the unsuccessful attacks on the Parliamentarian foot on the northern edge of Wash Common. A conservative total estimate might be about 600 men, giving a total casualty list of about 1,300, roughly equal to the losses suffered by Essex.

Most of the King's troops will have sought what comfort they could for the night with the expectation that the morning would see a resumption of the fighting, but unbeknown to them, Henry, Lord Percy, General of the Ordnance, was about to present the Council of War with a shattering report. He announced that, apart from the small quantities of powder still carried by the troops, the amount expended during the day had left supplies desperately short:

> ...we having not Powder enough left for halfe such another day, having spent four score barrells in it, three score more than had served the turne at Edgehill, nor could we be assured that the supply from Oxford of 100 Barrells more could come to us till the next day at noone...[4]

Surviving documents among the Royalist Ordnance Papers throw additional light on the crisis facing the King. So far as powder was concerned, the main shortages seem to have been in fine-grained powder for the use of the musketeers. However, as demonstrated by the King's despatch of the evening of the 20th to Sir John Heydon and other officers of the Ordnance Department in Oxford, there was also a serious lack of round shot for the artillery:

> ...our will and pleasure is And wee doe hereby require you immediately upon sight hereof to send unto us 50 Barrells of Powder with match and Bullett proportionable. And for the peeces of Cannon which wee have here 20 shot round. And for your soe doing this shalbe your warent. Given at oure Campe nere Newbury the 20th of September.
>
> To our trusty and welbeloved Sir John Heydon Lt. Gel. of Our Ordnance Sir George Stroad kt, and John Wandesford Esqr and to every of them
>
> Noted: Received this warrent betweene 7 and 8 at night.[5]

This order had obviously been despatched late in the afternoon, even before fighting came to an end, and it may be that the reference above to 100 barrels of powder refers to an additional request made later when the full extent of the depletion of supplies became apparent.

The situation was deemed sufficiently urgent for the intervention of the leading civilian official remaining in Oxford, Secretary of State Sir Edward Nicholas, who urged Heydon to:

> I pray use all possible expedicion in performing this his Majestie's command. I will presently send to the Gouvernor for the Powder, Bullett, and Match.

And I pray take Order for Carts and Carriages for the same, and the other things. I write in haste and rest
Yors to serve you

Ed: Nicholas
Oxon. 20 Sept. 1643

These things must needes goe away this night for Newbury.[6]

By 3 a.m. on the 21st, the convoy was on the road. A list of its contents survives, throwing much light on what munitions had been expended in the previous day's fighting, especially by the lighter guns which will have been employed in support of the infantry attacks:

> A Proportion of Powder, Shott Match and other provisions for the further furnishing of his Mats Artillery and Army for the present service. By warrant from his Maty. Dated 20th Setembris 1643 vizt

Di. Cannons – 40
Culverings – 40
Round shot 12 lb peeces – 60
For 6lb peeces – 140
Saker – 20
3lb peeces – 80
Horse Harneis for the Thill –13
For the Trace – 65
Tanned Hides – 9
From the Schooles Powder – 50 barrels
Match – 2 ton
Musket shott – 2[7]

Carried in a train of thirteen wagons, it would certainly have been well on in the day before the re-supply could reach the King's forces. Until it arrived, Charles and his commanders had the choice of either attempting to 'bluff it out', staying in position and hoping that the enemy would not mount a serious assault, or pulling back into Newbury leaving the road to Reading open to Essex.

The debate was apparently fierce. Rupert is reported to have favoured the army holding its ground, but he was outvoted. Sir John Byron was characteristically critical of the decision. Commenting that the day had ended 'with the advantage... extremely on our side', he went on to condemn its loss:

> By a very great error then committed, which was, that when we had beaten the enemy wholly from the ground we fought upon, so that not one of them appeared, and had possess ourselves of it, and drawne off a piece of their cannon, and might have done so by all the rest, had not our foot play'd the jades, and that intelligence was brought us of the great fright they were in, many of them stealing from their arms in the darkness of the night, we then upon a foolish and knavish suggestion of want of powder, quitted all our advantages, and about 12 o'clock at night drew off all our men as if we had been the beaten party, leaving to the enemy the field which from 6 o'clock in the morning till that time we had fought for and gained with the expense of so much good blood.[8]

The Royalist 'official' account tried to place a more positive interpretation on the decision, which was:

> ...in part to make a Bridge to a flying Enemy, lest indeed too great a despair of retreat might have made them opinionate a second fight in that disadvantageous place...[9]

It remains open to speculation whether a bold front on the morning of 21 September would have been enough to cause Essex either to despair or to pull back from his position in an attempt to find a way round the Royalist army. But the problem facing the Royalists was that without sufficient stocks of ammunition to keep their foot in action for long, they would have been in a very weak position to take advantage of such a move, and still less to beat off a determined attempt by the Parliamentarians to force their way through. In the circumstances, the decision to pull back into Newbury and revert to the former tactics of harassing the marching Parliamentarians by use of cavalry was probably the only realistic option open to the King.

Dawn on 21 September thus brought a welcome surprise for Essex and his men, who opened proceedings with a defiant discharge of artillery against what proved to be empty enemy positions. Some time was spent in surveying the battlefield, which provided a chilling reminder of the human cost of the fighting. Though one eyewitness commented that the evidence he saw suggested that the Royalists were unlikely to have lost more than about 500 men, Henry Foster spoke of reports of the Cavaliers carrying off during the night:

about 30 cart-load of maimed and dead men, as the towne-people credibly reported to us, and I think they might have carried away 20 cart-load more of their dead the next morning; they buried 30 in one pit, 14 lay dead in one ditch.[10]

On the Royalist side, on Enbourne Heath, Captain John Gwynne saw on the position occupied by the London Trained Band regiments 'a whole file of men, six deep, with their heads struck off with one cannon shot of ours.'[11]

With no time to spare to bury his dead, the Earl of Essex sent an instruction (unenforceable in the circumstances) to the Rector and Churchwardens of Enbourne:

> These are to will and require, and straightly command you forthwith in sight thereof, to bury all the dead bodies lying in and about Enborne and Newbury Wash, as you or any of you will answer to the contrary at his peril...[12]

It was reportedly at about 10 a.m. on 21 September that the Parliamentarians resumed their march. They followed the road to Reading south of Newbury, known in its initial stages as Monkey Lane, and then went across Greenham Common and through the villages of Brimpton and Aldermaston. Although Essex expected some sort of attempt by the Royalists to hinder his passage, at first they displayed little sign of activity. In the words of one Parliamentarian account:

> Col: Middleton with his own and three Regiments more (Lord Grey, Sheffield, Meldrum) and 200 commanded musquetiers under the command of Col: Barclay had the Rereguard. During which march the Enemy at a great distance shot from several hedges, but troubled us not. When we came to a long Heath [Greenham Common] we drew up the whole Army severall times, and no Enemy appeared.[13]

However Prince Rupert had no intention of allowing Essex to get away unmolested, and the Parliamentarians were shadowed by a force of horse under Lord Wilmot and the Earl of Northampton, who asked for the support of a party of commanded musketeers, quite probably from the force under Lisle and Wentworth. They saw their opportunity to attack as the Parliamentarians deployed to file along a narrow lane between the villages of Aldermaston and Padworth. As a Parliamentarian account admitted:

...at the entrance of a narrow lane toward Evening the enemy fell upon us with 800 commanded musquetiers and most of their horse, who caused our horse then in the rere to make a very disorderly and confused retreat. But when Col: Middleton with the rest of the Commanders in the rere hasted to charge the Enemy with our foot, he made them retreat with as much confusion over the Heath as they did us before: the losse not considerable on either side, but on the Enemies' most: Lieut. Browne was taken prisoner...[14]

According to a London newspaper account:

...we marched toward Reading (to gaine quarters to supply our want of victuals) and when we had marched 6 or 7 miles, the enemy's horse having got an advantageous passage, which our horse endeavouring to cleere, charged them, and in a narrow lane near Sir Humphrey Forster's house, part of our foote were disordered neere into a route by our owne horse for relief of which Col Middleton alights from his horse and draws out 60 musquetiers, which he valorously led up first to relieve a stout canonnier of ours, who with three men made good his station where he had charge of three case of drakes against all the enemy's horse, the King's horse were beaten off and 80 slain in the place with the loss of 10 of ours.[15]

Caught up in the confusion were Sergeant Henry Foster and his comrades. They were marching towards the rear of the Parliamentarian column when the Royalists:

...fell upon our reere in a narrow lane about a mile and a half from a village called Aldermason, they came upon us with a great body of foot and horse, our London Briggade marched in the reere, and a forlorn hope of 600 musquetiers in the reere of them besides a great number of our horse. But our horse which brought up the reere, durst not stand to charge the enemy, but fled, running into the narrow lane, routed our own foot, trampling many of them under their horses' feet, crying out to them: 'Away, away, every man shift for his life, you are all dead men', which caused a most strange confusion among us. We fired 10 or 12 Drakes at the enemy, but they came upon us very fiercely having their foot on the other side of the hedges; many of our wagons were overthrowne and broken: others cut their traces and horse-harnesse, and run away with their horses, leaving their wagons and carriages behind them: our foot fired upon the enemies' horse very bravely, and slew many of them; some report above 100 and not 10 of ours; some that we took prisoners our men were so enraged at them that they knockt out their braines with the butt-end of their muskets: in this great distraction and rout a wagon of powder lying in the way overthrowne some spark of fire or match fell among it, which did much hurt; 7 men burnt and 2 killed; the enemy had got 2 of our drakes in the reer, had not our foot played the men and recovered them againe: this was about 4 or 5 o'clock at night; many of our men lost their horses, and other things which they threw away in haste...[16]

Royalist accounts of what was apparently a near-disaster for their opponents are sketchy. Reporting the pursuit by the forces under Wilmot and Northampton, *Mercurius Aulicus* relates that:

...about three miles from Newbury towards Reading... Prince Rupert (who had three horses shot under him) giving them a fierce charge in their Reare, two of their Horse Regiments were routed and chased into their Foot, we doing good execution upon them for a farewell...[17]

This encounter was the last fighting of the day and indeed of the campaign. At about 10 p.m Essex's weary troops reached the village of Theale without further molestation.

King Charles, with most of his foot, had spent the day at Newbury. The King, who sat for an hour by the bedside of the dying Earl of Carnarvon, was shaken as the toll of casualties became apparent. Lord Falkland had still been missing at nightfall on 20 September and there were hopes that he had been taken prisoner. However with daylight his naked body, identifiable by a mole on his neck, was discovered. Clarendon paid a moving tribute to his dead friend:

...thus fell that incomparable young man, in the four and thirtieth year of his age, having so much despatched the business of life that the oldest rarely attain to that immense knowledge, and the youngest enter not into the world with more innocence; and whosoever leads such a life need not care upon how short warning it be taken from him...[18]

Also among the prominent Royalist dead were the young Earl of Sunderland, Colonel Sir Anthony Mansell of Sir William Vavasour's Brigade and Colonels Thomas Pinchbeck and Thomas Morgan.

Viewing the field, the Royalists saw ample evidence of what they regarded as Essex's hasty departure:

...they were forced to leave behind their heavy carriages, with many barrels of Musket and Pistoll Bullets, and very many Chirugeons Chests full of Medicaments. Some of the Cannon they buried is since taken up, and severall heapes of their dead were found cast into Wells, Ponds and Pits, one Draw-Well of 30 fathoms deepe being filled to the top with dead bodies, 8 or 9 whereof some of His Majestie's owne Troop tooke the paines to pull up, but left off the rest as not being able to endure the noisomenesse of the imployment; and in sundry places with armes and legges sticking out, besides those above ground whom they had not time to cover: great numbers of their maimed Officers and common men they left behinde...[19]

As had been the case after Edgehill, King Charles's sensitive nature recoiled in horror at the harsh realities of war. He issued a warrant to the Mayor of Newbury:

Our Will and Command is that you forthwith send unto the Townes and Villages adjacent, and bring hence all the sicke and hurt Souldiers of the Earle of Essex's Army, and though they be Rebels and deserve the punishment of Traytors, yet out of Our tender compassion upon them as being Our Subjects, Our Will and pleasure is that you carefully provide for their recovery, as well as for those of Our owne Army, and then to send them to Oxford...[20]

What this amounted to in practical terms is another matter. Certainly there were hospital facilities near Oxford for wounded Royalist troops, some of whom, if unfit for further service, would be sent home with the optimistic promise of receiving a pension from their parish. But it is difficult to imagine much care being taken of any Parliamentarian wounded who found themselves in the Royalist capital.[21]

Next day the Earl of Essex and his men found themselves free to resume their march without interference, as Rupert had called off the pursuit. The Parliamentarians entered Reading on 22 September, but made no attempt to garrison the town, marching on towards London, where Essex arrived three days later.

Whatever the private thoughts of many of the Parliamentarian leadership towards their Captain-General and his conduct of the campaign, it was necessary for propaganda purposes to proclaim a great victory. Essex publicly received the thanks of both Houses of Parliament and on 28 September, milking the situation to the full, his forces staged a triumphal entry into London. They were received at Temple Bar by the Lord Mayor and Aldermen

32 Captured Royalist standards. Cavalry cornets of both sides often bore political or religious slogans.

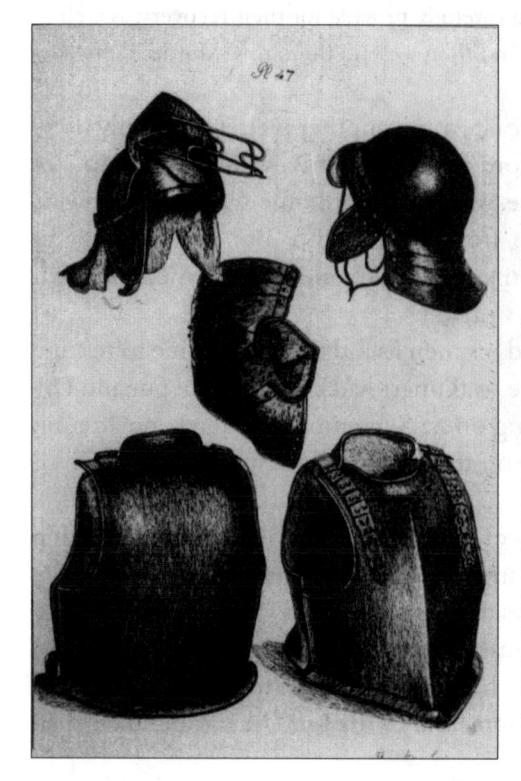

33 Back and breast plates. Most Parliamentarian body armour was manufactured in England, but in 1643 the Royalists were still importing considerable amounts from the Continent, leading to some variations in design. Apart from these, the opposing cavalry were armed and equipped virtually identically.

34 Unidentified Royalist cornet captured at Newbury. Motto: 'music, monarchy and harp'. Field: blue and red; fringe, white and red; devices, gold.

35 Cornet of Parliamentarian Captain Robert Mainwaring of the City of London Horse, captured at Newbury. Motto: 'Only in heaven'. Field: red; fringe, white and red; device, gold.

36 Units from London, including Phillip Skippon's troop of horse.

37 Cornet of Parliamentarian Captain John Weare, taken by Charles Gerard's forces at Newbury. Motto: 'For Peace and Truth'. Field: red; fringe, white and red.

38 Lucius Cary, Viscount Falkland (1610–43). Falkland, a moderate Royalist who had hoped that war could be avoided, was one of the King's Secretaries of State. He was increasingly depressed by the deepening and bitter war, and some contemporaries suggested that he deliberately sought his death at Newbury.

39 Parliamentarian cornet captured by Gerard's horse. It belonged to Captain Edwin Sandys, possibly of the Earl of Essex's Regiment of Horse. Motto: 'I hope to conquer'. Field: red; fringe, red and gold.

40 Royalist cornet taken at Newbury. Motto: 'long live the king'. Field: white; fringe, white and black.

41 Cornet of the Earl of Essex. Motto: (black on silver) 'Envy is a companion of virtue'. Field: tawney orange; fringe, tawney orange and white.

42 Cornet of Colonel Thomas Morgan, a Royalist colonel of horse killed by a cannon shot. Motto: 'Who is like God?'. Depicts St Michael slaying the dragon. Field: pale blue and red; fringe, white and red.

43 Oxford had been the Royalist capital since the end of 1642. It housed the King and his court, troops and numerous munitions and supply facilities.

44 Christchurch College, Oxford. Residence of King Charles I during his stay in the city.

Above left: 45 Royalist cornet taken at Newbury. Motto: 'square in every way' (in contrast to the 'Roundheads'). Field: white; fringe, white and black.

Above right: 46 Royalist cornet taken at Newbury. Motto: 'I live by these things: I die by these things'. Field: purple; fringe, purple and gold.

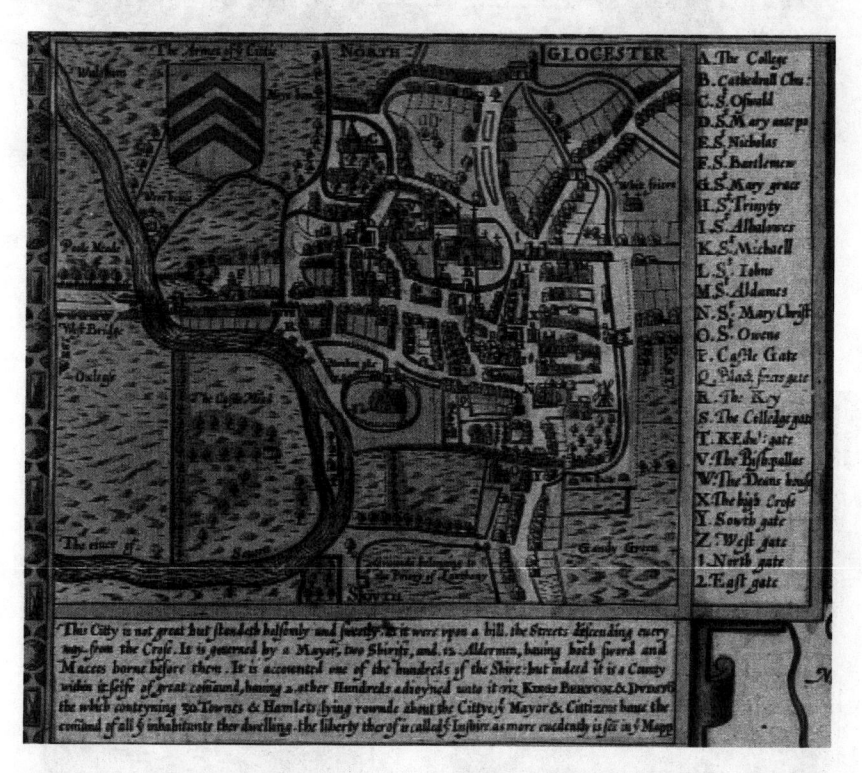

47 Gloucester, c.1611 (map by John Speed). Note the incomplete medieval fortifications.

48 Part of John Speed's Map of Berkshire, c.1611.

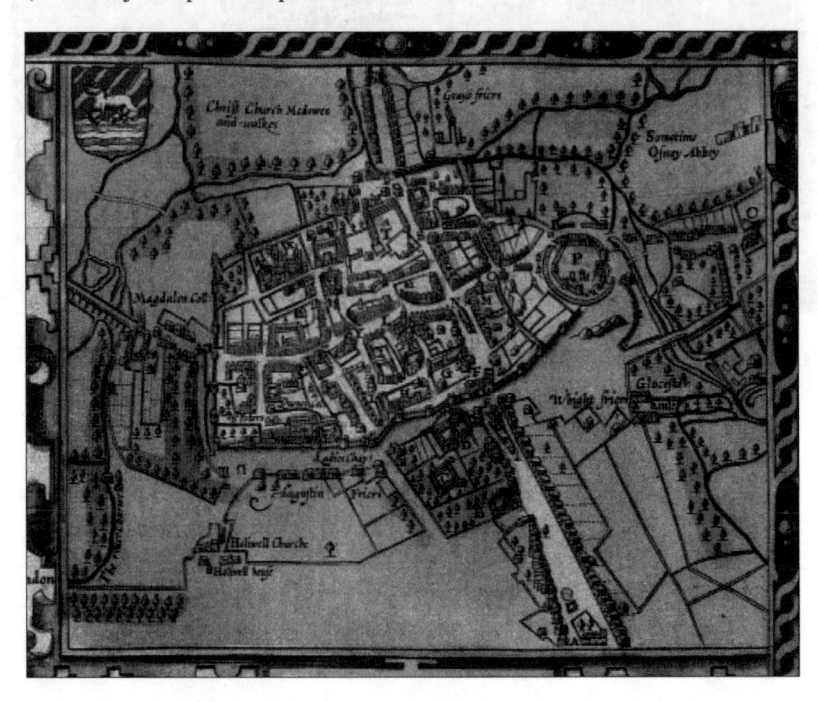

49 Oxford, c.1611 (map by John Speed). Much of the town still lay within its medieval walls, and its defences were further strengthened by rivers.

50 Round Hill viewed from the north. Marked by the prominent trees (centre right) Round Hill and the high ground running westwards from it (to the right in the photograph) dominated the northern half of the battlefield and saw some of the fiercest fighting.

51 The southern outskirts of Newbury viewed from the fields south of the River Kennet. The bulk of the Royalist army spent the night preceding the battle encamped on open ground beyond the hedgerow (centre). In the opening phase of the action Vavasour's Royalists advanced westwards across these fields against Robartes' Parliamentarians.

52 View westwards from the approximate point reached by Vavasour's advance looking towards the Parliamentarian position east of Skinner's Green Lane (behind hedgerow on horizon).

53 The high ground in the vicinity of Round Hill seen from the west from the approximate position of the London Brigade at the start of the battle.

54 View across Skinner's Green Lane towards Enborne Copse on the horizon, near which the Parliamentarian baggage train was parked.

55 Skinner's Green Farm. From here the Parliamentarian reserve advanced eastwards past Cope Hall (to the left of the photograph) in order to counter Royalist attacks.

56 The steep approach to Round Hill can be gauged in this photograph looking north-eastwards towards Skinner's Green.

57 The thick hedges and high banks which had an important influence on the nature of the fighting are still apparent in the lanes which cross the battlefield.

58 View south-westwards from Round Hill area towards the vicinity of Enborne Heath, where much of the cavalry action took place.

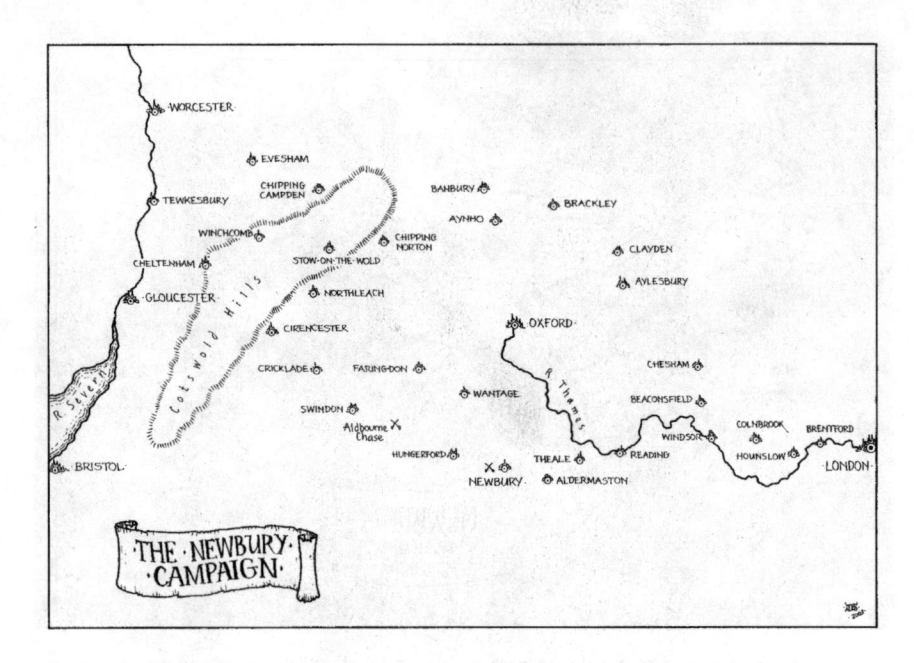

59 The Newbury Campaign.

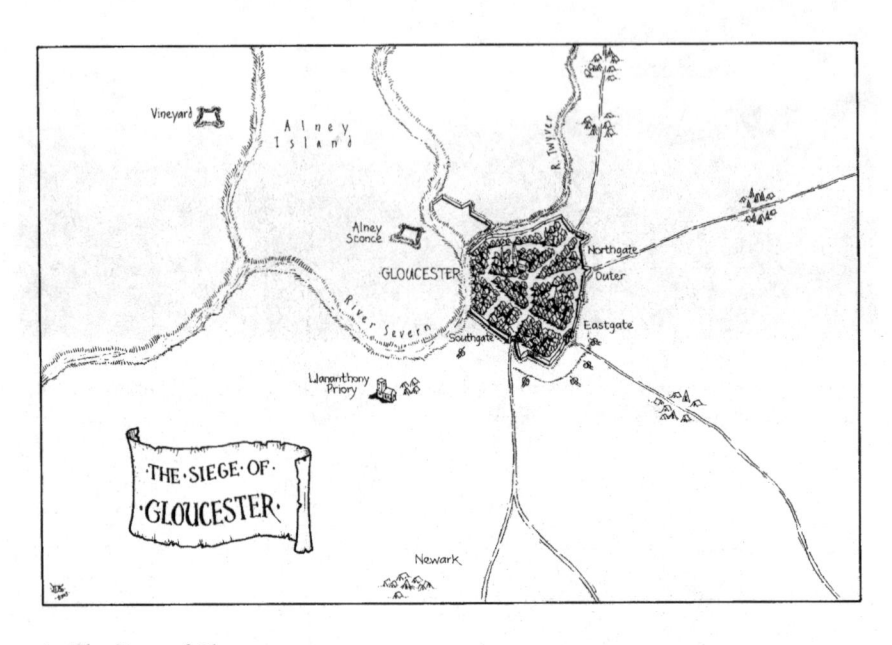

60 The Siege of Gloucester.

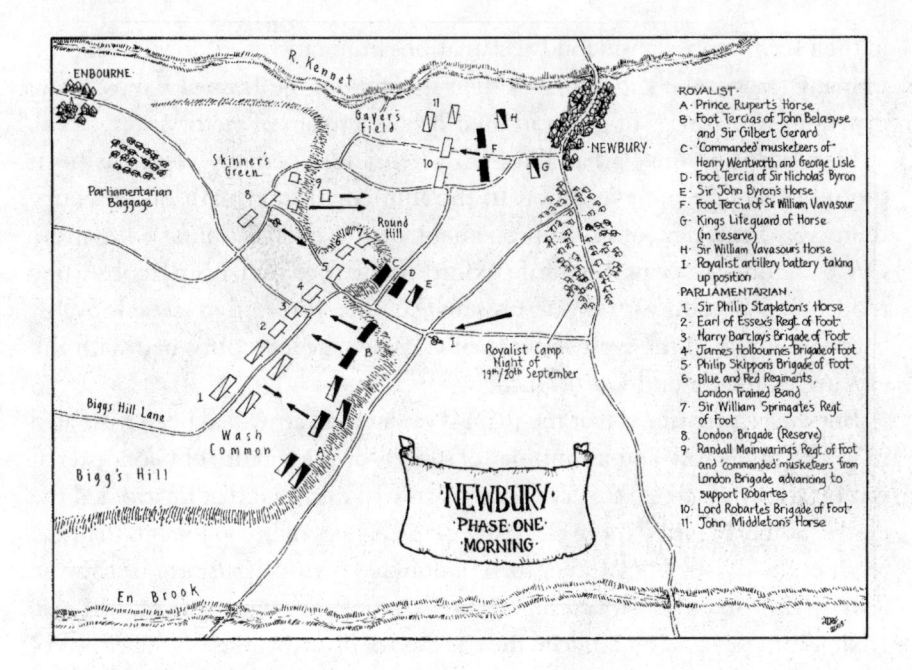

61 Newbury: Phase One.

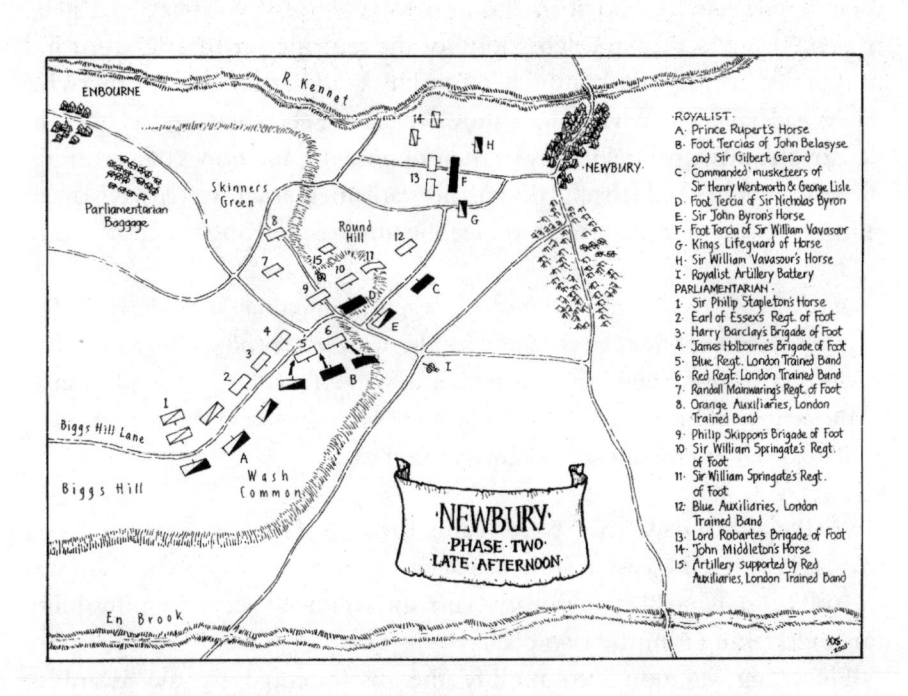

62 Newbury: Phase Two.

in their scarlet robes, amid loud acclamations from crowds of citizens, relieved in many cases at the safe return of their menfolk of the Trained Bands, many of whom wore sprigs of green in their hats as a token of victory.

How justified the Parliamentarian celebrations actually were has been the subject of debate ever since. In the immediate aftermath of Newbury there was little sign of an improvement in the overall military situation. On 3 October a strong body of Oxford Army foot under Sir Jacob Astley reoccupied Reading without resistance and refortified it as a Royalist garrison, while in the west the tide of Cavalier success continued with the capture of Exeter and Dartmouth.

But the fact remained that the main Royalist field army had been frustrated in its design of crowning its summer of success by the capture of Gloucester. It can be argued that Essex's success was narrowly won, and that he avoided the destruction of his army more as a result of the failings of his opponents than as a result of his own abilities. Other than undoubted personal gallantry, he showed few signs of inspired generalship at any stage of the campaign, and the real credit for the success, and indeed the survival, of his army rests on the efforts of some of his subordinates, notably Skippon, John Middleton and their brigade commanders, as well as on the endurance and fighting spirit of their men.

But while the Parliamentarians could find cause for qualified satisfaction, their opponents had no such grounds for comfort. Newbury might be presented as a victory in celebrations for the returning army at Oxford and in Royalist propaganda, but the King and his commanders knew otherwise. They had failed in what might prove to have been their best chance to destroy the principal field army of their opponents, and hopes of a crushing victory which would bring down the Parliamentarian 'war party' lay in ruins. As Clarendon described the feeling among the King's supporters:

> upon the King's return to Oxford, there appeared nothing but dejection of mind, discontent, and secret mutiny; in the army, anger and jealousy among the officers, every one accusing another of want of courage and conduct in the actions of the field; and they who were not of the army, blaming them all for their several failings and gross oversights...[22]

Both Rupert and Wilmot were blamed for the failure to prevent Essex from relieving Gloucester, and each accused the other. The siege itself was the subject of general criticism, with no one willing to accept responsibility for undertaking it in the first place.

The King attempted to mollify the discontented by the award of honours to some of those prominent in the successes of the summer.

There was a baronetcy for Sir John Byron, a dukedom for Prince Rupert, a knighthood for Colonel Michael Woodhouse and promotion for Charles Gerard, though significantly nothing for Lord Wilmot. None of this did anything to dilute the bitterness, which would continue into the winter and beyond, with Rupert eventually quitting the venomous atmosphere of the Court to take up a new command in Wales and its borders.

Certainly neither King Charles nor any of his senior commanders emerge from the Newbury campaign with any credit. Charles himself failed to impose any order among the quarrelling factions in his Council. His professional soldiers, especially it would seem the Earl of Forth, underestimated the difficulties of capturing Gloucester, and overestimated the strength and morale of a Royalist army still suffering from the effects of its heavy losses a few days earlier in the storming of Bristol. Although the task was a more difficult one than admitted, Rupert's and Wilmot's attempts to halt Essex's relief force were seem to have been ineffectual and rather half-hearted.

The tale of blunders and missed opportunities continued during Essex's return march to London. Royalist pursuit in the first few vital hours was slow and hesitant, the blame this time lying with Forth and the King, rather than with Rupert, who seems to have recovered much of his verve and fierce energy. Yet the Prince, having imposed an invaluable delay on the Parliamentarians in the action at Aldbourne Chase, so allowing the Royalists to reach Newbury first, then squandered his advantages by his failure to reconnoitre and occupy key ground.

As a result the Royalists were forced to fight an offensive action in circumstances which largely favoured the enemy. As for their opponents, it was largely a 'soldiers' battle' in which the higher command played little part, although Rupert evidently fought with his customary fierce courage. Such laurels as came the Royalist way rested with more junior commanders, in particular Nicholas and John Byron, but these were not enough to win the day.

With the failure at Newbury still rankling, the Royalist Council of War met on 29 September in the gracious surroundings of Oriel College, Oxford. They can have little appreciation of these surroundings as they pondered the situation which now faced them. London was beyond their reach and, with the looming threat of intervention on the side of Parliament by the Scots, the English troops about to arrive from Ireland were likely largely to be absorbed in efforts to counter its effects. The only offensive of consequence planned would be by a newly-created and, as it would prove, inadequate army, under Lord Hopton. This was to advance into Sussex and Kent and, rather optimistically, to 'point towards London'.

Though few yet realised it or were willing to admit it, the Royalists had lost the initiative. Far more significant than the deliberations at Oriel College was the ratification on 25 September of the Solemn League and Covenant between Parliament and the government in Scotland, which in a few months would bring a powerful Scottish army to the assistance of the King's English opponents. The Parliamentarian Bulstrode Whitlocke wrote of Newbury: 'All were Englishmen… and pity it was that such courage should be spent in blood of each other.'[23] Thanks to the failure of either side to win a decisive victory there, the English, Welsh, Scottish and Irish subjects of all of King Charles' Three Kingdoms would henceforth play a bloody price in a steadily widening and deepening war.

Notes

CHAPTER 1

1. Earl of Clarendon, *History of the Rebellion and Civil Wars in England*, VII, 149
2. *ibid*, 150
3. *ibid*, 152
4. *ibid*, 155
5. *ibid*, 176
6. *ibid*, 157
7. Quoted Atkin and Loughlin, *Gloucester and the Civil War*, 171
8. Clarendon, *op. cit.*, VII, 158
9. Warburton, *Memoirs of Prince Rupert and the Cavaliers*, II, 266
10. *ibid*, 276
11. *ibid*, 278
12. Clarendon, *op. cit.*, VII, 158
13. *Lords Journal*, VI, 127
14. Gardiner, *History of the Great Civil War*, I, 183–4

CHAPTER 2

1. Corbett, *An Historical Relation of the Military Government of Gloucester*, 11
2. *ibid*
3. Bodleian Library, *Tanner MS* 66, f.197
4. Atkin, *op. cit.*, 46. Suggests as many as 30,000
5. Clarendon, *op. cit.*, VII, 162
6. *ibid*, 164
7. *ibid*
8. Domer, *Life of the Earl of Essex*, 215–7
9. *Royalist Ordnance Papers*, Item 146, 264–5
10. *ibid*, Item 155, 269
11. Clarendon, *op. cit.*
12. *Royalist Ordnance Papers*, Item C12, 365
13. Domer, *op.cit.*, 216
14. John Gwynne, *Memoirs*, 21
15. Corbett, *op. cit.*, 54
16. Quoted Young, Peter and Emberton, Wilf, *Sieges of the Great Civil War*, 40. It has also been suggested that the verse has its origin in the explosion of the great Royalist mortar mentioned earlier.
17. Quoted Atkin, *op. cit.*, 172
18. Corbett, *op. cit.*, 45
19. Domer, *op.cit.*, 233
20. *Bibliotheca Gloucestrensis*, 280
21. *Lords Journal*, VI, 190

22	*Mercurius Aulicus*, 28 August 1643, 473
23	Foster, *A True and Exact Relation of the Marchings of the Two Regiments of the Trained Bands of the City of London*, 1
24	Bod. Lib., *Tanner MS* 62, ff.293–4
25	Foster, *op. cit.*, 1
26	*ibid*
27	*ibid*
28	*ibid*
29	*ibid*
30	Foster, *op. cit.*, 3
31	*ibid*, 4
32	*ibid*, 2
33	*Mercurius Aulicus*, 492
34	Foster, *op. cit.*, 4
35	*ibid*
36	*ibid*, 5
37	Warburton, *op. cit.*, 286–7
38	*ibid*
39	Foster, *op. cit.*, 5
40	*ibid*
41	*ibid*
42	Corbett, *op. cit.*, 46

CHAPTER 3

1	Clarendon, *op. cit.*, VII, 174
2	*ibid*
3	*ibid*
4	*ibid*, 176
5	*ibid*, 177
6	*ibid*
7	*Mercurius Aulicus*, 498
8	*ibid*
9	*ibid*, 499–500
10	*True and Impartial Relation of the Bataille betwixt His Majestie's Army and that of the Rebels Neare Newbury in Berkshire*
11	Foster, *op. cit.*, 7
12	*Mercurius Aulicus*, 514–5
13	*ibid*
14	Foster, *op. cit.*, 8
15	Foster, *op. cit.*, 8
16	Foster, *op. cit.*, 7
17	*ibid*
18	Bod. Lib., *Clarendon MS*
19	Barratt (ed.), *The Journal of Prince Rupert's Marches*, 10
20	Foster, *op. cit.*, 8–9
21	Barratt, *op. cit.*
22	John Gwynne, *Memoirs*, 36–7

23	Foster, *op. cit.*
24	Warburton, *op. cit.*, 289
25	*ibid*, 290
26	*ibid*
27	*True and Impartial Relation of the Bataille…*, 2
28	Foster, *op. cit.*, 8
29	*Clarendon MS*
30	*True and Impartial Relation of the Bataille…*
31	*ibid*
32	Foster, *op. cit.*
33	*ibid*
34	Foster, *op. cit.*, 9
35	*ibid*

CHAPTER 4

1	Clarendon, *op. cit.*
2	*ibid*, VIII, 12
3	*ibid*

CHAPTER 5

1	*Clarendon MS*
2	*ibid*
3	British Library, *Additional MS* 18980, f.97
4	*True and Impartiall Relation of the Bataille…*, 4
5	Clarendon, *op. cit.*, VII, 210
6	Money, *Battles of Newbury*, 37, quoting Vicars, *Parliamentary Chronicle*
7	The best analysis of the somewhat complicated and uncertain composition of Essex's foot may be found in Peachy, Stuart and Turton, Alan, *Old Robin's Foot*, Southend-on-Sea, 1987.
8	Foster, *op. cit.*, 3
9	*ibid*
10	*True and Impartiall Relation of the Bataille*, 4
11	*ibid*
12	H.M.C. Portland MS, I, 713
13	See Barratt, *Cavaliers*, 194–5
14	*DNB*

CHAPTER 6

1	Foster, *op. cit.*, 7
2	*ibid*
3	Foster, 5
4	*ibid*
5	*ibid*
6	Brit. Lib., *Harleian MS* 6804, f.92
7	Foster, *op. cit.*, 6
8	*ibid*
9	Whitlocke, Bulstrode, *Memorials of English Affairs*, 71
10	Clarendon, *op. cit.*

11	Brit. Lib., *Add. MS* 18980, f.97
12	*Clarendon MS*
13	*ibid*
14	Clarendon, *op. cit.*, VII, 23
15	Aubrey, John, *Brief Lives*, 87
16	*Clarendon MS*
17	*Mercurius Aulicus*, 26 September 1643
18	Foster, *op. cit.*, 7
19	*Harleian MS* 6804, f.92
20	*Clarendon MS*, 1738
21	*True and Impartiall Relation of the Bataille*, 5
22	John Gwynne, *Memoirs*, 46
23	Foster, *op. cit.*
24	*ibid*
25	*ibid*, 7
26	*Harleian MS* 6804, f.92
27	Codrington, *Life of Robert Devereux, Earl of Essex*, 33; Foster, *op. cit.*, 7

CHAPTER 7

1	Foster, *op. cit.*, 8
2	*ibid*
3	*Mercurius Aulicus*, 21 September 1643
4	Foster, *op. cit.*, 7
5	*Royalist Ordnance Papers*, Item 183
6	*ibid*
7	*ibid*
8	*Harleian MS* 6804, f.92
9	Foster, *op. cit.*, 8
10	*ibid*
11	John Gwynne, Memoirs, 47
12	Quoted Money, *Battles of Newbury, op. cit.*, 63
13	Foster, *op. cit.*, 8
14	*ibid*
15	*Mercurius Britannicus*
16	Foster, *op. cit.*
17	*Mercurius Aulicus*, 21 September 1643, 529–30
18	Clarendon, *op. cit.*, VIII, 234
19	*Mercurius Aulicus*
20	*ibid*
21	See Barratt, John, *Cavaliers*, 76–8
22	Clarendon, *op. cit.*, VII, 238
23	Whitlocke, *op. cit.*, 71

Appendix: Order of Battle

THE PARLIAMENTARIAN ARMY
Captain-General: Robert Devereux, 2nd Earl of Essex
Lieutenant-General of Horse: Sir Philip Stapleton
Major-General of Foot: Philip Skippon
General of Ordnance: Sir John Merrick

HORSE
Around 6,000 men organised into two 'wings' under Stapleton and Colonel John Middleton:

SIR PHILIP STAPLETON'S WING
Strength, June–August (excluding officers)
Earl of Essex's Lifeguard (raised 1642)	–
Earl of Essex (r.1642)	391
John Dalbier (r.1642)	219
Sir James Ramsey (r.1642)	–
Edmund Harvey (r.1643)	500?
Arthur Goodwin (r.1643)	586
James Sheffield (r.1642)	275
Richard Norton (r.1643)	–
Sir Samuel Luke 3 troops	

JOHN MIDDLETON'S WING
John Middleton (r.1643)	343
Lord Grey of Groby (r.1643)	–
Sir John Meldrum (r.1642)	–
Earl of Denbigh (r.1643)	–
Hans Behr (r.1643)	–

FOOT
Around 8,000 men

HARRY BARCLAY'S BRIGADE
Strength (excluding officers)	*July/Aug*	*December*
Harry Barclay (redcoats)	496	138
John Holmstead (redcoats)	416	89
Thomas Tyrell	450	127

JAMES HOLBOURNE'S BRIGADE

James Holbourne	290	111
Francis Thomson	351	81
George Langham (bluecoats?)	431	80

LORD ROBARTES' BRIGADE

Lord Robartes (redcoats)	365	188
Sir William Constable	365	142
Francis Martin	250	85

PHILIP SKIPPON'S BRIGADE

Philip Skippon (redcoats)	516	161
Sir William Brooke	–	–
Henry Bulstrode	376	110

LONDON BRIGADE
Red Regiment (Lieutenant-Colonel Robert Davies)
Blue Regiment (Lieutenant-Colonel Francis West)
Red Auxiliary Regiment
Blue Auxiliary Regiment (Colonel John Warner)
Orange Auxiliary Regiment
Randell Mainwaring (redcoats)
The regiments of the London Brigade probably each averaged about 900 men

UNBRIGADED
Strength July–August, (excluding officers)

Earl of Essex (Lieutenant-Colonel John Bamfield, orange coats)	726
Sir William Springate (redcoats)	–

DRAGOONS
150 men
Captain Jeremiah Abercromby's company
Captain Cornelius Shibborne's company

ARTILLERY
At least two demi-culverin and over twenty lighter pieces.

THE ROYALIST ARMY
Captain-General: King Charles I
General of Horse: Prince Rupert
Lieutenant-General of Horse: Henry, Lord Wilmot
Major-General of Foot: Sir Jacob Astley
General of the Ordnance: Henry, Lord Percy
Lieutenant-General of Ordnance: Sir John Heydon

HORSE
About 7,000, probably divided into 5 brigades under Charles Gerard, Sir John Byron,

the Earl of Carnarvon, Prince Rupert and Lord Wilmot, although the composition of each brigade is unknown. The following regiments are known to have been present:

King's Lifeguard (r.1642) (Lord Bernard Stuart), two troops
Prince Rupert (r.1642) (Lieutenant-Colonel Dan O'Neill), c.500 men
Prince Rupert's Lifeguard (r.1642) (Sir Richard Crane), 150 men
Queen's Regiment (r.1643) (Colonel Lord Jermyn; Lieutenant-Colonel John Cansfield), c.300 men
Lord Wilmot (r.1642) (Lieutenant-Colonel Edward Feilding (killed))
John Belasyse (r.1643) (Major Paul Smith)
Lord Digby (r.1642) (Lieutenant-Colonel Thomas Weston)
Henry, Lord Percy (r.1643) (Lieutenant-Colonel Lancelot Holtby)
Earl of Carnarvon (r.1642) (Lieutenant-Colonel Matthew Holdrish)
Prince of Wales (r.1642) (Lieutenant-Colonel Sir Thomas Byron)
Earl of Northampton (r.1642) (Lieutenant-Colonel Charles Compton)
Sir Arthur Aston (r.1642) (Lieutenant-Colonel George Boncle)
Lord Chandos (r.1642) (Lieutenant-Colonel Christopher Sawyer)
Sir John Byron (r.1642) (Lieutenant-Colonel. Sir Francis Butler)
Sir Thomas Aston (r.1642)
Sir John Urry (r.1643)
Sir Charles Lucas (r.1643)
Thomas Morgan (r.1643) (Morgan killed 'with a field piece')
Charles Gerard (r.1642)
Sir George Vaughan (r.1643)
Sir Thomas Tyldesley (r.1642) (Lieutenant-Colonel Thomas Dalton (killed); Captain Thomas Whittington (killed))
Sir William Vavasour (r.1643)
Lord Spencer (r.1643)
Sir Nicholas Crispe (r.1643)
James Hamilton (r.1643)
Lord General (r.1642) (Lieutenant-Colonel Sir Adrian Scroop)
Lord Andover (r.1642)
Prince Maurice (r.1642) (Lieutenant-Colonel Guy Molesworth)
William Eure (r.1643)

FOOT
About 7–8,000

SIR NICHOLAS BYRON'S TERTIA
King's Lifeguard (r.1642, redcoats) (Lieutenant-Colonel William Leighton), c.500 men
Prince of Wales (r.1643, bluecoats) (Colonel Michael Woodhouse), 700 men
Lord General (r.1642, redcoats) (Lieutenant-Colonel Herbert Lunsford)
Charles Gerard (r.1642, bluecoats) (Lieutenant-Colonel Edward Villiers)
Sir Lewis Dyve (r.1642) (possibly a detachment from Abingdon garrison)
Thomas Blagge (r.1642) (possibly a detachment from Wallingford garrison)
Lord Grandison (r.1642)
Sir Lewis Kirke (r.1643?) (possibly a detachment from Oxford garrison)

JOHN BELASYSE'S TERTIA
John Belasyse (r.1642) (Lieutenant-Colonel Sir Theophilus Gilby)
Richard Bolle (r.1642)
Sir Ralph Dutton (r.1642) (Lieutenant-Colonel Stephen Hawkins)
Sir Jacob Astley (r.1642) (Major Toby Bowes)
Prince Rupert (r.1642, bluecoats) (Lieutenant-Colonel John Russell)

SIR GILBERT GERARD'S TERTIA
Sir Gilbert Gerard (r.1642) (Lieutenant-Colonel Ratcliffe Gerard)
Lord Molyneux (r.1642) (Lieutenant-Colonel Roger Nowell), c.200 men
Sir Thomas Tyldesley (r.1642) (Lieutenant-Colonel Hugh Anderton; Captain Thomas Singleton and William Butler, killed), c.200 men
John Stradling (r.1642)
Sir Charles Lloyd (r.1642, redcoats)
Richard Herbert (r.1642) (Major Edward Williams)
John Owen (r.1642) (Lieutenant-Colonel Roger Burgess)
Anthony Thelwell (r.1642)
Lord Rivers (r.1642) (Lieutenant-Colonel John Boys)
Thomas Pinchbeck (r.1643) (Pinchbeck mortally wounded)
Lord Percy (r.1643) (Lieutenant-Colonel Henry Bard)
William Eure (r.1643) (Lieutenant-Colonel William Martin)
Conyers Darcy (r.1643)

SIR WILLIAM VAVASOUR'S TERTIA
Sir William Vavasour (r.1643) (Lieutenant-Colonel John Treherne)
Lord Herbert (r.1643) (Colonel Edward Somerset)
Samuel Sandys (r.1643) (detachment from Worcester garrison?)
Sir Anthony Mansell (Trained Band)
Richard Bassett (Trained Band)
Richard Donnell (Trained Band)

'Commanded' musketeers (Colonel Henry Wentworth and Lieutenant-Colonel George Lisle): 1,000 men detached from regiments at Bristol

DRAGOONS
Prince Rupert (r.1642) (Colonel Thomas Hooper)
Henry Washington (r.1642)
Lord Wentworth (r.1642)
Sir Robert Howard, two troops

ARTILLERY
20 guns*

---

*Details drawn from Reid, Stuart, *Officers and Regiments of the Royalist Army*; Peachey, Stuart and Turton, Alan, *Old Robin's Foot*; and Turton, Alan, *The Chief Strength of the Army*.

Bibliography

PRIMARY SOURCES

Barratt, John (ed), *Prince Rupert's War: the Journal of Prince Rupert's Marches (1642–46)*, Birkenhead, 1995.
Bibliotheca Gloucestrensis: A collection of scarce and curious tracts relating to the County and City of Gloucester, Parts I and II, Gloucester and London, 1823.
Bodleian Library: *Clarendon MS* 1738 (Sir John Byron's account).
British Library: *Additional MS* 18980 (account of anonymous Royalist officer); *Harleian MS* 6804 (papers of Royalist Council of War).
Clarendon, Earl of, *History of the Rebellion and Civil Wars in England*, Oxford, 1888.
Codrington, Robert, *Life of Robert Devereux, Earl of Essex*, London, 1646.
Corbett, John, *An Historical Relation of the Military Government of Gloucester*, London, 1645.
Domer, Robert, *Life of the Earl of Essex*, London, 1647.
Foster, Henry, *A True and Exact Relation of the Marchings of the Two Regiments of the Trained Bands of the City of London*, London, 1643.
Mercurius Aulicus, Oxford, 1643.
Roy, Ian (ed), *The Royalist Ordnance Papers, 1642–46*, Parts I and II, Oxfordshire Record Society, 1964 and 1975.
True and Impartial Relation of the Bataille betwixt His Majestie's Army and that of the Rebels Neare Newbury in Berkshire, Oxford 1643 (the Royalist 'official' account, often attributed, on no certain evidence, to Lord Digby).
True relation of the Late Expedition of His Excellency Robert Earle of Essex for the Relief of Gloucester, London, 1643.
Tucker, Norman (ed), *Military Memoirs: the Civil War* [Captain John Gwynne], London, 1967.

SECONDARY SOURCES

Appleby, David, *Our Fall Our Fame: The Life and Times of Sir Charles Lucas*, Newtown, 1996.
Atkin, Malcolm and Loughlin, Wayne, *Gloucester and the Civil War: a City Under Siege*, Stroud, 1992.
Barratt, John, *Cavaliers: the Royalist Army at War, 1642–46*, Stroud, 2000.
Barratt, John, 'King Charles 1st's Lifeguard of Foot', in *Military Illustrated*, No. 54.
Gardiner, S.R, *History of the Great Civil War*, London, 1893.
Money, Walter, *The Battles of Newbury*, 2nd ed., London, 1884.
Newman, Peter, *Biographical Dictionary of Royalist Officers, 1642–1660*, New Jersey, 1981.
Peachey, Stuart and Turton, Alan, *'Old Robin's Foot': the equipping and campaigns of Essex's Infantry, 1642–45*, Southend-on-Sea, 1987.
Reid, Stuart, *All the King's Armies: A Military History of the English Civil War, 1642–*

1651, Staplehurst, 1998.
Reid, Stuart, *Officers and Regiments of the Royalist Army*, Southend-on-Sea, n.d.
Roberts, Keith, *First Newbury 1643*, Oxford, 2003.
Roberts, Keith, *Matchlock Musketeer, 1588–1688*, Oxford, 2002.
Roberts, Keith, *Soldiers of the English Civil War: Infantry*, Oxford, 1991.
Tincey, John, *Ironsides: English Cavalry, 1588–1688*, Oxford, 2002.
Tincey, John, *Soldiers of the English Civil War: Cavalry*, Oxford, 1991.
Turton, Alan, *The Chief Strength of the Army: Essex's Horse, 1642 1645*, Southend-on-Sea, 1992.
Warburton, Eliot, *Memoirs of Prince Rupert and the Cavaliers*, London, 1849.
Young, Peter, *Edgehill 1642*, Kineton, 1967.
Young, Peter, 'Order of Battle of the Parliamentarian and Royalist Armies at the First Battle of Newbury', in *Journal of the Society for Army Historical Research*, 1964.

List of Illustrations

1. Bristol Castle. Courtesy of Jonathan Reeve.
2. 'Cavaliers and Roundheads'. JR414b22p1307 16001650. Courtesy of Jonathan Reeve.
3. Parliamentarian newsbook. JR420b22p1380 16001650. Courtesy of Jonathan Reeve.
4. Ludlow Castle. Courtesy of Jonathan Reeve.
5. Robert Devereux, Earl of Essex (1591–1646). JR699b34fp78 16001650. Courtesy of Jonathan Reeve.
6. Westminster. St Stephen's Chapel and Westminster Hall. JR274b10p1116 16001650. Courtesy of Jonathan Reeve.
7. John Pym (1584–1643). JR680b22p1276 16001650. Courtesy of Jonathan Reeve.
8. Sir Jacob Astley (1579–1652). JR681b22p1280 16001650. Courtesy of Jonathan Reeve.
9. The key Parliamentarian garrison of Kingston upon Hull. Courtesy of Jonathan Reeve.
10. Rioting soldiers. Courtesy of Jonathan Reeve.
11. Contemporary illustration depicting the variety of dress and equipment among troops. Courtesy of Jonathan Reeve.
12. A musketeer. JR290b10p1166 16001650. Courtesy of Jonathan Reeve.
13. Contemporary cartoon of an English soldier in Ireland. JR698b21p467 16001650. Courtesy of Jonathan Reeve.
14. Contemporary print possibly depicting dragoons firing from horseback. Courtesy of Jonathan Reeve.
15. Cornet of Captain Vivers of Arthur Goodwin's Regiment of Horse (Parliamentarian). Author's collection.
16. Cornet of Lieutenant-Colonel John Cansfield of the Queen's Regiment of Horse (Royalist). Author's collection.
17. Royalist cornet captured at Cirencester. Author's collection.
18. Cornet of Major William Boswell (Spencer's Horse) taken at Cirencester. Author's collection.
19. Cornet of Royalist Major Christopher Wormsley (Sir Nicholas Crispe's Regiment of Horse), killed at Cirencester. Author's collection.
20. Musket. Tempus Archive.
21. Musket drill. Courtesy of Jonathan Reeve.
22. Harquebusiers as depicted in John Cruso, 'Militarie Instructions for the Cavalerie', 1635. Author's collection.
23. Title page of a popular contemporary drill book. Author's collection.
24. Pike drill. Courtesy of Jonathan Reeve.
25. Infantry Equipment. Author's collection.
26. Contemporary images of soldiers. JR288b10p1164 16001650. Courtesy of Jonathan Reeve.

27	Contemporary woodcut of the Army Council of 1647. Tempus Archive.
28	Prince Rupert (1619–82). Courtesy of Jonathan Reeve.
29	Wooden effigies of soldiers. JR286b10p1162 16001650. Courtesy of Jonathan Reeve.
30	Lord Robartes (1606–65). Author's collection.
31	A variety of Civil War soldiers. Courtesy of Jonathan Reeve.
32	Captured Royalist standards. JR695b21p330 16001650. Courtesy of Jonathan Reeve.
33	Back and breast plates. Author's collection.
34	Unidentified Royalist cornet captured at Newbury. Author's collection.
35	Cornet of Parliamentarian Captain Robert Mainwaring of the City of London Horse, captured at Newbury. Author's collection.
36	Units from London, including Phillip Skippon's troop of horse. Courtesy of Jonathan Reeve.
37	Cornet of Parliamentarian Captain John Weare, taken by Charles Gerard's forces at Newbury. Author's collection.
38	Lucius Cary, Viscount Falkland (1610–43). Courtesy of Jonathan Reeve.
39	Parliamentarian cornet captured by Gerard's horse. Author's collection.
40	Royalist cornet taken at Newbury. Author's collection.
41	Cornet of the Earl of Essex. Author's collection.
42	Cornet of Colonel Thomas Morgan, a Royalist colonel of horse killed by a cannon shot. Author's collection.
43	Oxford, the Royalist capital from the end of 1642. JR712b31p534 16001650. Courtesy of Jonathan Reeve.
44	Christchurch College, Oxford. Residence of King Charles I during his stay in the city. Author's collection.
45	Royalist cornet taken at Newbury. Author's collection.
46	Royalist cornet taken at Newbury. Author's collection.
47	Gloucester, c.1611 (map by John Speed). Author's collection.
48	Part of John Speed's Map of Berkshire, c.1611. Author's collection.
49	Oxford, c.1611 (map by John Speed). Author's collection.
50	Round Hill viewed from the north. Author's collection.
51	The southern outskirts of Newbury viewed from the fields south of the River Kennet. Author's collection.
52	View westwards from the approximate point reached by Vavasour's advance. Author's collection.
53	The high ground in the vicinity of Round Hill seen from the west. Author's collection.
54	View across Skinner's Green Lane towards Enborne Copse on the horizon. Author's collection.
55	Skinner's Green Farm. Author's collection.
56	Photograph looking north-eastwards towards Skinner's Green. Author's collection.
57	The thick hedges and high banks, which had an important influence on the nature of the fighting, are still apparent in the lanes which cross the battlefield. Author's collection.
58	View south-westwards from Round Hill area towards the vicinity of

List of Illustrations

	Enborne Heath. Author's collection.
59	The Newbury Campaign. Drawn by Derek Stone. Author's collection.
60	Map of the Siege of Gloucester. Drawn by Derek Stone. Author's collection.
61	Newbury: Phase One. Drawn by Derek Stone. Author's collection.
62	Newbury: Phase Two. Drawn by Derek Stone. Author's collection.

Index

Adderbury, 32

Addington, 32

Adwalton Moor, battle of (1643), 12

Aldbourne Chase, action at (1643), 64-9, 77

Aldermaston, 116

Alvescot, 62, 63

Armies, 71-7

Ashburnham, John, 63

Astley, Major General Sir Jacob, 25, 72, 80, 110, 136

Aston, Sir Arthur, 17,
    Regiment (H) (R), 100

Aston, Sir Thomas, 101, 103-4
    Regiment (H) (R), 91, 103-4

Banbury, 58

Barclay, Colonel Harry, 88, 105, 106-7, 110, 116

Bassett, Colonel Richard, 96
    Regiment (F) (R), 90

Beaconsfield, 30

Behr, Colonel Hans,
    Regiment (H) (P), 57

Belasyse, Colonel John, 91, 105, 106
    Regiment (F) (R), 91, 109

Bigg's Hill, 87, 88

Bigg's Hill Lane, 87, 88, 99

Blackwell, Colonel Thomas,
    Regiment (F) (R), 91

Blagge, Colonel Thomas
    Regiment (F) (R), 90, 109

Blue Auxiliary Regiment (LTB) (F) (P), 87

Blue Regiment (LTB) (F) (P), 58, 87, 105, 107-9

Bolles, Colonel Richard
    Regiment (F) (R), 91, 109

Boteler [Butler}, Major, 105

Brackley Heath, 30-1

Bristol, 12-13, 22, 36, 37, 56, 136

Broadway Hill, 61

Brookes, Colonel Sir William,
    Regiment (F) (P), 87, 105

Bulstrode, Colonel Henry
    Regiment (F) (P), 87

Burford, 63

Byron, Sir John, 12, 62, 66, 84-5, 100, 101-5, 106, 110, 112, 114-5, 136
    character and early career, 90-1
    Regiment (H) (R), 91

Byron, Sir Nicholas, 90, 101, 104-5, 110

Carnarvon, Robert Dormier, Earl of, 15, 92, 99, 118
    Regiment (H) (R), 100

Chalgrove, action at (1643), 11, 92

Charles I, King, 10, 13, 22, 110, 118, 136
    and relief of Gloucester, 36
    character of, 78-9

Cheltenham, 36, 60

Chillingworth, Dr John, 2, 7-8

Chipping Norton, 32

Chisledon, 63

Cirencester, 21, 60-1, 62, 63

Colnbrook, 30

Constable, Sir William
    Regiment (F) (P), 86

Cricklade, 61, 64

Crispe, Sir Nicholas
    Regiment (H) (R), 60-1

Cromwell, Oliver, 20

Dalbier, Colonel John
    Regiment (H) (P), 97

Darcy, Colonel Conyers,
    Regiment (F) (R 0, 91

Dark Lane, 103, 104

Dartmouth, 136

Deddington, 31-2
Denbigh, Basil Feilding, Earl of,
  Regiment (H) (P), 68, 86
Digby, Lord George, 63, 67
Donnell, Colonel Richard
  Regiment (F) (R), 90
Donnington Castle, 83
Draper, Captain, 98
Dutton, Colonel Sir Ralph
  Regiment (F) (R), 91, 109
Dyve, Colonel Sir Lewis,
  Regiment (F) (R), 90, 109
Eastern Association, 15
Enbourne, 69, 83, 84, 86, 89, 96, 116
Enbourne Heath, 84-88, 96, 100, 116
Enbourne, River, 83
Essex, Robert Deveraux, Earl of,
  10, 72, 84, 88, 109-10, 116
  and relief of Gloucester, 30-2
  character, 81
  march to Newbury, 58-69
  Lifeguard (H) (P), 32, 35, 73, 85
  Regiment (F) (P), 60, 68, 87, 105, 106
  Regiment (H) (P), 32, 35, 97
Essex's Army, 19-20, 29-30, 80
  deployment of at Newbury, 86-7
Eure, Colonel William,
  Regiment (F) (R), 91
Evesham, 59
Exeter, 14, 136
Fairfax, Lord Ferdinando, 12
Fairfax, Sir Thomas, 12
Fairford, 62
Falkland, Lucius Cary, Earl of, 72, 80, 101-3, 118
Faringdon, 62, 64
Forest of Dean, 16, 26, 27
Fortescue, Lieutenant Colonel, 86
Forth, Patrick Ruthven, Earl of, 23, 36, 39-40, 62, 72, 78-9, 110, 136
Foster, Henry, 30-1, 36-7, 62-3, 68, 89, 95, 107-9,

111, 112, 115, 117-9
Gainsborough, action at (1643), 20
Gerard, Colonel Sir Charles, 92, 136
  Regiment (F) (R), 90, 101, 105
Gerard, Colonel Sir Gilbert, 91, 105, 106
  Regiment (F) (R), 91
Gloucester, 39-40, 56, 136,
  description of, 21
  reasons for Royalist attack on, 16-17
  relief of, 37-8,
  siege of, 24-30
Goodwin, Colonel Arthur
  Regiment (H) (P), 57, 97
Grandison, Lord, 17
  Regiment (F) (R), 90, 105
Greenham Common, 116
Grey of Groby, Lord
  Regiment (H) (P), 29, 35, 65, 68, 86, 116
Gwynne, Captain John, 27, 62-3, 106, 116
Henrietta Maria, Queen, 19, 25
Hamstead, 69, 88
Hamstead Park, 87
Harvey, Colonel Edmund, 34, 87,
  Regiment (H) (P), 34, 65, 87, 97
Herbert, Colonel Richard
  Regiment (F) (R), 91, 109
Hertford, William Seymour, Marquis of, 12, 13
Heydon, Sir John, 25, 113
High Wycombe, 19
Highnam, battle of (1643), 21
Holbourne, Colonel James, 87, 105, 106-7
  Regiment (F), (P), 87
Holmestead, Colonel John
  Regiment (F) (P), 87
Hopton, Sir Ralph (later Lord), 12, 13, 36, 137
Hopton Castle, 90
Hull, 12, 15
Hungerford, 64, 65, 69
Hyde, Edward, (later Earl of Clarendon), 14, 16-18, 56-7, 102

Index

Jermyn, Lord Henry, 67
Kennett, River, 69, 83, 86, 89, 95
King's Life Guard (F) (R), 90, 105
King's Life Guard (H) (R), 90
Kirke, Sir Lewis, 100
Langham, George, 87
Lansdown, battle of (1643), 12
Lechlade, 62
Legge, Major William, 17-8, 25
Letton, 61
Lichfield, 11
Lisle, Colonel George, 62, 75, 92, 99, 101, 116
Lloyd, Colonel Sir Charles
    Regiment (F) (R), 91, 106
London, 10, 15, 19, 29, 83, 111
London Trained Bands (London Brigade), 29, 30, 32-3, 36-7, 57, 61, 71, 86-7, 95, 105, 116
Lord General's Regiment (F) (R), 90, 105
Lucas, Sir Charles, 99
Mainwaring, Colonel Randell
    Regiment (F) (P), 29, 87, 106-7
Mansell, Colonel Sir Anthony, 118
    Regiment (F) (R), 90
Marrow, Major John, 34
Martin, Colonel
    Regiment (F) (P), 88
Massey, Colonel Edward,
    as Governor of Gloucester, 21-2
    attitude towards Royalists, 17-18
    character and early career, 17
Maurice, Prince, 12, 15, 60
    Regiment (H) (R), 99
Meldrum, Colonel Sir John,
    Regiment (H) (P), 65, 116
Middleton, Colonel John, 30-1, 81
    Regiment (H) (P), 65, 67, 72, 86, 96, 116-7, 136
Molyneux, Captain Presland, 18
Molyneux, Richard, Lord
    Regiment (F) (R), 91
Monkey Lane, 105, 116

Morgan, Colonel Thomas, 118
    Regiment (H) (R), 91
Newbury, 63, 69, 88, 111, 116
    description of , 83-4
Newcastle, William Cavendish, Earl of, 12, 15, 91
Nicholas, Sir Edward, 113
Northleach, 63
Norton, Colonel Richard,
    Regiment (H) (P), 68, 97
Orange Auxiliary Regiment (F) (P), 87
Owen, Colonel John
    Regiment (F) (R), 91, 109
Owen, Susan, 58
Oxford, 10, 11, 19, 56, 78, 81
Oxford Army 13,
    after fall of Bristol, 14-5
    strength of, 22
    at Newbury, 77-80
    deployment of, 89-92
    losses, 112
Padworth, 116
Painswick, 17, 39
Percy, Lord Henry, 24, 26, 78, 80, 113
    Regiment (F) (R), 91
Pinchbeck, Colonel Thomas, 118
    Regiment (F) (R), 91
Plymouth, 14
Prestbury, 36
Price, Colonel Herbert, 91
Prince of Wales' Regiment (F) (R), 64, 79, 90, 101, 105
Pye, Colonel Sir Robert, 61
Pym, John, 18, 20
Queen's Regiment (H) (R), 34, 57, 87-8
Ramsay, Colonel Sir James,
    Regiment (H) (P), 32, 34, 39, 97
Reading, 3, 64, 81, 83, 84, 105, 114, 116, 136
Red Auxiliary Regiment (LTB) (F) (P), 87, 99, 105
Red Regiment (LTB) (F) (P), 30, 87, 105, 107-9, 111
Richmond, James Stuart, Duke of, 64, 78

Rivers, Earl
   Regiment (F) (R), 91
Robartes, John, Lord, 86, 95, 96, 99, 110
   Regiment (F) (P), 86
"Round Hill", 83, 84, 85, 87, 89, 90, 91, 95, 99,
   101-5, 111
Roundway Down , battle of, (1643), 12, 19
Rupert, Prince, 11, 12, 17-19, 27, 78, 85, 92, 95, 98,
   101, 104, 106, 110, 112, 114, 118
   character and early career, 13, 79
   wishes to storm Gloucester, 23
   and Essex's relief of Gloucester, 32
   march to Newbury, 61-69
   responsibility for Royalist failure, 35-6, 56, 136
Sandys, Colonel Samuel
   Regiment (F) (R), 90
Scotland,
   alliance with Parliament, 20, 137-8
Severn, River, 21
Sheffield, Colonel Thomas,
   Regiment (H) (P), 34, 65, 68, 116
Sheldon, Captain, 100
Siege engines, 27-8
Skinner's Green, 87
Skinner's Green Lane, 88, 89, 98, 103, 105
Skippon, Major General Philip, 71, 81-2, 88, 89, 95,
   104-5, 106, 110-16
   Regiment (F) (P), 87
Smith, Major Paul, 100
Spencer, Lord, 16, 28
   Regiment (H) (R), 60-1
Springate, Colonel Sir William
   Regiment (F) (P), 86
Stamford, Earl of
   Regiment (F) (P), 22, 23, 28
Stamford in the Vale, 62
Stapleton, Colonel Sir Philip, 30, 35, 81, 94, 98
   Regiment (H) (P), 68, 86, 87, 97

Stow on the Wold, 32
Stradling, Colonel John,
   Regiment (F) (R), 91
Sudeley Castle, 39
Sunderland, Earl of, 118
Swindon, 62, 63
Tewkesbury, 59
Theale, 84
Thelwell, Colonel Anthony,
   Regiment (F) (R), 91
Thompson, Colonel Francis,
   Regiment (F) (P), 87
Throckmorton, Baynham, 26
Tyldesley, Sir Thomas,
   Regiment (F) (R), 91
Tyrell, Colonel Thomas
   Regiment (F) (R), 87
Urry, Sir John, 34, 64-5, 67, 72
Vavasour, Colonel Sir William, 17, 22, 64, 89, 95,
   96, 100
   Regiment (F) (R), 90
Vieuville, Marquis de, 67-9
Villiers, Lieutenant Colonel Edward ("Ned"),
   101, 104
Wales, 16
Waller, Sir William, 12, 19-20, 21, 111
Wantage, 64, 69
Wash Common, 84, 85, 92, 95, 96, 100, 105, 106,
   107-9, 111, 112
Washington, Colonel Henry
   Regiment (D) (R), 92
Wentworth, Thomas, Lord, 92, 101, 116
Western Royalist Army, 12-15
Wilmot, Henry, Lord, 12, 32, 35, 56, 57, 72, 80, 92,
   100, 110, 116, 118, 136-7
Winceby, action at (1643), 20
Winchcombe, 57
Woodhouse, Colonel Michael, 64, 77, 90, 101, 136

TEMPUS REVEALING HISTORY

The Great Siege of Chester
JOHN BARRATT
£16.99
0 7524 2345 2

The Battle for York: Marston Moor 1644
JOHN BARRATT
£16.99
0 7524 2335 5

If you are interested in purchasing other books published by Tempus,
or in case you have difficulty finding any Tempus books in your local bookshop,
you can also place orders directly through our website

www.tempus-publishing.com